TRILLION-DOLLAR MOM$

MARKETING TO A NEW GENERATION OF MOTHERS

MARIA T. BAILEY
BONNIE W. ULMAN

Dearborn™
Trade Publishing
A **Kaplan Professional** Company

This publication is designed to provide accurate and authoritative information in regard to the subject matter covered. It is sold with the understanding that the publisher is not engaged in rendering legal, accounting, or other professional service. If legal advice or other expert assistance is required, the services of a competent professional should be sought.

President, Dearborn Publishing: Roy Lipner
Vice President and Publisher: Cynthia A. Zigmund
Acquisitions Editor: Michael Cunningham
Senior Managing Editor: Jack Kiburz
Interior Design: Lucy Jenkins
Cover Design: Design Solutions
Typesetting: the dotted i

Published by Dearborn Trade Publishing
A Kaplan Professional Company

Printed in the United States of America

05 06 07   10 9 8 7 6 5 4 3 2 1

Library of Congress Cataloging-in-Publication Data

Bailey, Maria T.
    Trillion-dollar moms : marketing to a new generation of mothers /
Maria T. Bailey and Bonnie W. Ulman.
        p. cm.
    Includes bibliographical references and index.
    ISBN 1-4195-0457-6 (hardcover)
        1. Women consumers—United States.   2. Mothers—United States.
3. Marketing—United States.   4. New Age Consumers—United States.
I. Ulman, Bonnie W.   II. Title.
HF5415.33.UB35 2005
658.8'3'0852—dc22

                                                                                2004028760

DEDICATIONS

Maria T. Bailey: To my husband, Tim, and my children, Morgan, Keenan, Owen, and Madison: Above and Beyond

Bonnie Ulman: To my parents, Morgan and Linda Worthy, who always made me believe I could do anything . . . and still do; and to Alan, Madison, and Jacob, who make it all count

Contents

It took two individuals with a shared interest and passion to write this book but it also required the support of others. We would like to thank these individuals who helped us as individuals and as a duo as we took on this herculean task.

Thanks first to Dearborn Trade Publishing for its forward thinking about the opportunity to market products to mothers. It has been a pleasure working with Michael Cunningham, Jack Kiburz, and the team at Dearborn. We never would have met Michael had it not been for Jennifer Bayse Sander, author of *Wear More Cashmere,* and one of the smartest people in publishing.

Thank you to all those who gave of their time to be interviewed by Bonnie and Maria. We sought out the most uniquely qualified professionals to share with us their insights but in doing so we had to ask very busy people to share precious time with us. We greatly appreciate your support in this project.

Now for the individuals who have touched us separately while writing this book.

There's a wonderful old proverb about traveling with the right person on a trip. I definitely have had the best traveling companion for this journey. Thank you, Maria, for setting an extraordinarily high but not unreachable standard for those who have the pleasure of working with you. We're all the better for it. This journey would not have begun or been completed without the support and assistance of a great many people who deserve more than an acknowledgment.

To my husband, Alan, who shows us every day that fathers are just as important as mothers. Thank you for stepping up during this project. I thank my children, Madison and Jacob, who made me a mother—something I always wanted—and who show me every day why even the challenging moments are worth it. Your curiosity about why the world works the way it does inspires me to keep asking "Why?"

Thank you to the team at The Haystack Group—Stefanie, Holly, Renee, Jeffri, Tationya, and Kyli—for guarding an environment that makes work fun and allows each of us to pursue our next big idea. Your ideas, support, and guidance were invaluable. And to Dennis, a special thank-you for knowing just when it was time for the caffeine. A special thank-you to Dalia Baseman Faupel, who served so many roles in the development of this book—editor, critic, cheerleader, and, most important, friend. How you do what you do amazes me. I sincerely appreciate the clients of Haystack who often inquired about the progress of the book, demonstrated tremendous patience, and never made me feel guilty for "checking out." My heartfelt gratitude to Pat McBurnette and the team at Moore & Symons research for always running into the fire when I yelled "Help!" Your contributions for the quantitative research for this book are invaluable. Thank you to my friends—at work and home—who never roll their eyes when I announce, "I have an idea!"

I am grateful to have such remarkable women (and men) in my life. A special thank-you goes to friend and colleague Debbie Wetherhead, who, in addition to running her own company and mothering two daughters, never failed to ask me how it was going. Finally, to the individuals who shared their wisdom and insights about a new generation of mothers, about marketing to mothers, and about being mothers—thank you. What you had to say made our ideas real.

Thanks to Carter Auburn for all your inspiration and support. You define the word *friend,* and sharing this experience with you is something that was totally unexpected in many ways but valued every day. One day I hope I can adequately express my appreciation. One day!

I remember the first time Bonnie and I met over the phone. The call lasted for more than an hour and to anyone outside of marketing, it may have sounded alien. In fact, many marketers would have looked perplexed. We tossed our insights and thoughts on moms back and forth, covering everything from consumer behavior to attitudinal changes. Over the years, we've debated almost every aspect of motherhood, and what you hold in your hand is the shared passion we have for the topic of marketing to moms. I am grateful not only for the professional relationship that we have built but also for the friendship that has grown out of working together. It's been a lot of fun.

To the team at BSM Media and those who support BlueSuitMom™, Mom Talk Radio™, and *Today's BlueSuitMom* every day, thank you for making the dream come true. Thanks also to all the moms who participate in BSM's Mom Mind Pool and give us access to what moms like and dislike around the clock. Your insights are invaluable to our knowledge of the Mom Market. Thank you to Joyce K. Reynolds, Molly Gold, Nancy Cleary, Natalie Gharmann, Jorj Morgan, Karen Deerwester, Marti Zenor, Valika Schivcharran, and Roni Leidermann, who make up the team behind all we do at BSM Media. Thank you to my right-hand woman and good friend, Laura Motsett, who keeps me together. Thanks to Judene Hartzell for everything. To Tammy Harrison, your commitment and friendship is something I truly value. Special thanks to Rachael Bender, BlueSuitMom's cofounder, who gives nothing short of everything to marketing to moms.

Thank you to my business associates Kevin Burke, John King, and Jennifer Sparks at Lucid Marketing. It's a pleasure to work with you. To Delia Passi, CEO of Medelia Communication, you are one of the smartest businesswomen I know; it has been a great learning experience working with you. I thank Barbara Litrell, our mutual friend, for connecting us with each other.

Finally, to all of our wonderful clients who share our passion for marketing to moms, I think it's this shared spirit that makes our work so much fun. We are truly blessed to work with the greatest brands and companies around the world.

I find that in one's daily life there are people who listen to your dreams, weather your complaints, and cheer you on. It's not often that you get to thank these individuals publicly so I would like to do so now. To my running buddies, Melodi Fehl, Kim Peeler, and Renee Gould, thank you. In particular, thank you to Christine Gerbracht, who will always go an extra mile with me regardless of my pace. Thank you to Ellen Jacobs, Kathy Tight, Diane Hanke, Alyce White, Rita McCann, Nancy DeJohn, Valerie Rodriquez, Leslie Withrow, and Sue Courtade, who are my village of support as a mom. To Jennifer Calhoun and Brenda Kouwenhoven, thank you for all the years of friendship and laughter. Thank you to Audrey Ring for being a great friend every day no matter where it takes you.

Thank you to my parents, Bill and Susan Telli, and Jackie Alligood and the late Dr. H. Michael Alligood. I am what I am today because of these four people. Thank you also to my in-laws, Patrick and Patricia Bailey, who always show interest in everything I do. Thank you to my siblings, Debbi Telli Jackson, Mike Redington and sister-in-law Maureen Redington, Bryan Redington, Michael Alligood, and Mathew Alligood, who stay close regardless of where we all are traveling in our lives.

And finally, to my husband Tim, who cooks farmer dinners when I'm traveling, manages homework, and juggles activity schedules by himself so that I can follow my dreams. Thank you in particular for the pen and legal pad to write on when Hurricane Frances knocked out our electricity and computers a week before this book was due. Thank you is not enough to express my appreciation. To the four people who make my job as a mom the best one I have. Madison, Owen, Keenan and Morgan, my little marketing gurus who can evaluate a commercial in less time than it takes them to change a DVD. You are the reason for everything I do in life. Thank you for being the best kids in the world.

Mothers represent the most powerful consumers in the United States today. Each year they control more than $1.6 trillion in household spending. That's more than the Gross Domestic Product (GDP) of Australia, South Africa, and the Philippines.[1] Their purchasing power can make or break the shelf life of a product, the market penetration of a new brand, or the growth of Fortune 100 companies. They can even sway a presidential election as soccer moms were credited with doing in the 1996 election of Bill Clinton. In fact, suburban mothers represented one-fifth of all votes cast in elections from 1982 to 1996.[2]

Sales of some products are obviously driven by mom purchases: food, children's clothing, and household items. A closer look at mom spending, however, uncovers even larger items, including transportation, financial services, travel, and real estate. The extended network of spending that mothers represent increases the mom value to companies looking for growth in sales and customer retention. If you continue on her path of spending, you will discover that she is buying personal hygiene products for the male in her life, home improvement items, and health care for aging parents. In this role she makes stops at the grocery store, purchases prescriptions, and finds health care for her extended family members. Her involvement in school PTAs, nonprofit organizations, and athletic teams places her in a position to make buying decisions for everything from carnival rides and baseballs to books and banking services. Finally, after all her work is done on the home front, moms are off to the office where they are buying computers, furniture, financial services, paper, and pens. Working mothers are also employing people, producing revenue, and fueling the economy. The bottom line is that moms are spending money, and they are doing it all day long in many different places for many different people.

The lifetime value of a mother and the consumers she influences creates an immense opportunity for businesses. It's amazing to us that there are still industries, companies, and brands that have yet to tap the Mom Market. Instead, we watch companies run after the niche du jour, which finds itself in the headlines of marketing publications. Veteran marketers pursue new markets to find growth opportunities to meet demanding sales goals with reduced budgets. They will spend thousands, sometimes millions, trying to learn the behavior of these groups, such as Gay and Lesbian and Asian-American markets, but neglect to look at the numbers. No other segment of consumers can deliver the spending that the Mom Market can contribute to their bottom line. We recommend that instead of dashing off to a new segment in search of the silver bullet, you as marketers examine the potential of the Mom Market and evaluate the way in which you have been trying to tap it.

Why would anyone ignore such a powerful consumer group? It's a question we contemplate every time we find ourselves in the position of convincing a CMO or brand manager that moms mean business for them. In a time when companies are struggling to meet sales goals and find new areas of growth, the Mom Market presents great opportunities. The numbers speak for themselves:

- According to the latest study in 2000 of the U.S. Department of Agriculture (USDA), a family with an average income will spend $165,630 on a child by the time the child reaches 18 years of age.[3]
- According to 2000 figures from the Department of Agriculture, the agency that tracks family expenditures, parents with incomes of $38,000 to $64,000 spent $18,510 on miscellaneous items for the average child from birth through

the age of 18. This includes spending on entertainment, reading material, VCRs, summer camp, and lessons.[4]

- Females outnumber males in the United States by more than 6 million (roughly 6 percent), with a significant percentage having at least one child. There are 141,606,000 women with children in the United States.[5]
- There are 6.2 million women-owned businesses.[6]
- Women-owned businesses generate $1.15 trillion in sales.[7]
- Women-owned businesses employ 9.2 million people.[8]

So how is it that two women become so passionate about one subject? It may have something to do with our firsthand knowledge of the market based on our roles as mothers and consumers. Or it could be, more importantly, that the marketer in each of us dislikes seeing opportunities remain untapped in the marketplace. In any case, we consider ourselves very fortunate to be able to merge our personal roles with our professional endeavors.

Maria entered motherhood as swiftly as a good marketing campaign can move a product. As the mother of three children under two years of age, she learned quickly the spending requirements of a mom. After two decades of a business career that included working at *The Miami Herald,* Discovery Zone, and AutoNation, she launched BlueSuitMom.com™, the award-winning Web site designed for working mothers. Today her company, BSM Media, is an internationally recognized marketing firm specializing in connecting companies with the Mom Market. Additionally, BSM Media owns and produces Mom Talk Radio™, BlueSuitMom.com, *Today's BlueSuitMom* magazine, and Mom's Mind Pool, a think tank of moms that provides clients with 24/7 access to marketplace behaviors and insights. Her reputation in the area of work and life balance is recognized by *Inc.* magazine, who named her one of the best resources in America. Since inception, the team at BSM Media has worked with more than 100 companies, from Fortune 100 brands to start–ups, developing marketing strategies, designing creative campaigns and Web sites, and producing original content and conducting training programs. Maria's role as Blue-SuitMom's founder, host of Mom Talk Radio, and columnist in numerous mom-targeted publications, gives her unique 24/7 access to the issues and trends in the Mom Market. Her first book, *The Women's Home-Based Business Book of Answers* (Prima, 2001), established her as a trusted resource in the woman business owner and momprenuer segments. Her second book, *Marketing to Moms: Getting Your Share of the Trillion-Dollar Market* (Prima, 2002), was the first to examine the spending power of mothers and how companies can tap the spending of the lucrative mothers. Maria is a media resource on issues related to women in business, female consumerism, and moms. She's been featured in *The New York Times, The Wall Street Journal, Women's Day,* and *Smart Money* and appears in numerous television interviews across America, including CNBC. Audiences who hear her speak are not surprised to learn that she is also a marathon runner. The energy, dedication, and passion she has for connecting companies with the opportunities in the Mom Market transcends the walls of any room. It is her commitment to delivering the best insights possible to marketing professionals that led her to Bonnie Ulman.

Ask Bonnie a question and she'll likely respond with one of her own. Calling herself the "kid who never stopped asking why," she is passionately curious about what motivates consumers to think and act as they do. Her journey began by conceiving and implementing award-winning programs for top consumer brands, making a name for herself as she secured awareness for her clients and helped them address brand and business challenges. But she found herself hungry for more information about the consumers she was creating messages to reach, and she began exploring new ways to bring these individuals to life. Bonnie was among the first to develop unique methods to bring the traditional advertising-based discipline of account planning to public relations. Creating her own team to delve into consumer behavioral research, she shook up the norm and achieved spectacular results for clients in all sectors. At the same time, as a new mother, she began looking for ways to achieve more balance in her life. With a firm foundation of consumer research behind her plans, she opened her own consumer behavioral research consultancy in 2000, The Haystack Group. Creating an environment where questions are welcomed and working mothers find the flexibility they need, the Haystack team established a reputation among blue-chip clients. Using nontraditional and traditional research methods alike, The Haystack Group approach defined a bull's-eye target consumer for clients, unearthed important insights for reaching these consumers, and developed communication strategies that torpedoed the proverbial clutter. With client demand growing, Haystack expanded offerings to include brand strategy, public relations, and employee communications. Bonnie's journey to expertise in the Mom Market, like Maria's, began after the birth of her children and evolved as she began to understand how motherhood had changed her and the other mothers she knew, as people and as consumers. A sought-after expert on the topics of consumer research, brand strategy, and marketing to mothers, Bonnie contributed to Maria's most recent book, *Marketing to Moms*. Because of her insatiable curiosity for how moms make decisions and spread the word about brands they like and those they don't, she can often be found hypothesizing and preparing to test a new theory about moms after a visit to her daughter's school, a Starbucks run, or whenever she talks to Maria.

Over lunch one day we were sharing insights with each other about shifts we were seeing in the behavior of mothers. Discussing the Mom Market was nothing new with us. In fact, we have a difficult time separating our work from reality, observing moms in restaurants, at airports, and even in public restrooms. On this day, however, we focused our conversation on the generational differences of mothers and the emergence of Gen X and Y moms. We pondered research both had conducted, program responses, and behavioral characteristics. By the end of the exchange, we knew that the insights we could provide to marketers and their companies would be groundbreaking and useful in tapping the spending of moms. What you hold in your hands is the result of lunch that day and many hours of market immersion. We hope it will provide you with the tools you need to increase sales, acquire and retain customers, and build your brand.

What you will find in this book is an accumulation of proprietary research, experiential insights, and documented facts about the Mom Market. The interviews took place both in person and via telephone nationally as well as through an online survey conducted among 500 mothers and grandmothers who live in the Southeast, Northwest, and Midwest, and on the West Coast with incomes of $50,000 and more. The survey was conducted through leading research firm Harris Interactive. Survey respondents were categorized by age in traditional generational cohorts, Gen Y 1977–1994, Gen X 1964–1976, Baby Boomers 1946–1964, and Silver Birds 1935–1945. These women included both stay-at-home mothers and moms who work outside the home.

In writing this book, we not only wanted to give you the whys but the hows when it comes to understanding moms and their purchasing decisions. As the title suggests, there is a new generation of mothers in the marketplace. They are new in terms of their defined generational cohort, as Gen Xers continue to grow their families and Gen Ys age to become new moms. The Baby Boomer market also presents a new generation as these older moms begin to take on the characteristics of the mothers who share the same age of child. You'll soon learn that it's more about the age of the child than the age of the mother when you are marketing to her parental consumer needs. To gain a good understanding of where these mothers are from a generational prospective, we will examine each in depth, noting along the way the marketing techniques that best motivate them to purchase your product. Additionally, we will take a quick glimpse at the changing face of today's grandmothers, which we call Silver Birds. With 25 million mothers in the workplace, companies must now also market themselves to mothers as prospective employers. To retain the best female employees who also happen to be mothers, it is more necessary than ever for companies to sell themselves as the employer of choice. For this reason, we will discuss in our dissection of generations, the work ethics of each group of mothers. Armed with a clear understanding of the Mom Market as it is comprised today, we will then examine individual marketing strategies. Our goal is to empower you with the knowledge you need to execute a marketing plan that will successfully tap the Mom Market. We will do this by revealing new research, presenting case studies, and including the insights of some of America's most well-respected business leaders. We intend this book to be one that you refer to often as a resource. In addition, we extend an invitation to you to contact us at http://www.trilliondollarmoms.com for additional information, insights, or comments.

Mention the word *mom* to just about anyone and he or she will conjure up an image that is as individual as the person you are questioning. The mental picture they draw will likely be based on interactions with their own mother. Few things are as constant in life as having a mother, aside from dying and paying taxes. We all have a mother whether we maintain a close relationship or not, and we have a visual image of what we believe a mother looks like. Perhaps one of the greatest obstacles for marketers as they look toward marketing to mothers is how to erase their personal images of mothers. We ask you to release any mental pictures or impressions you might be using as a benchmark for your marketing strategies. Let yourself start fresh for at least the next 14 chapters as we dissect a mom in a way that has never been done before. There are lots of pieces to assemble to create the most accurate picture of today's Mom

Market. A clean slate will enable you to more fully appreciate not only the way she thinks, acts, and ultimately purchases, but, more importantly, the why behind it. Ultimately, your open-mindedness will allow you to apply our findings in creative ways to the goals your company establishes in the Mom Market. Once we've told you all we know, you can combine this new information with your own experience, intuition, and market data to produce a marketing plan that increases sales.

Some books are written to inspire, others to motivate. This one we hope will empower you with the tools, insights, and knowledge to tap the Mom Market. The opportunities that moms present to you and your company are endless. Let's begin on our journey to capture the trillion-dollar market of a new generation of mothers.

1

TAKING AIM AT
THE MOM MARKET

"If you always do what you've al-
ways done, you'll always get what you've always gotten." Everyone has their favorite sayings, and this one is ours. We find it
particularly fitting in the context of marketing to moms. For
marketers today who try to utilize the same techniques they've
used for generations and generations, the returns will be far
less than what they have achieved previously. Unfortunately,
too many companies are stuck in this rut, still executing old advertising and promotion techniques, wondering why they are
not increasing market share or sales. These frustrated industry
professionals soon find themselves chasing what we refer to as
"the niche of the month." The catalyst could be the Bureau of
the Census or another government agency releasing figures on
a new growing demographic and suddenly the pages of *Brand
Week* or *DM News* are filled with articles on how brands X, Y, and
Z are all launching programs to capture this new emerging
market. Operating with no long-term strategy, they jump feet-

first into the "niche of the week" marketing when, in fact, few if any niche markets can compare to the size of the Mom Market. Why are these marketers ignoring a consumer group whose spending exceeds all others? Our guess is twofold. First, they have not achieved the results they wanted in the Mom Market and therefore have moved in another direction, hoping to discover the silver bullet that will increase sales and make up for the lack of activity in the mom sector. If you find yourself in this category, you've taken the first step in getting back on track with mothers.

Second, we feel that they are ignoring the Mom Market because they think they are hitting it with their marketing using female strategies. Although it is true that all moms are women, not all women are moms, and expecting to connect with a mom as you speak to her only as a woman is a well-documented misnomer. According to our research, moms are 80 percent more likely to buy a product from a company that recognizes the multiple roles she plays in her life. By ignoring her role as a mother and just speaking to her as a woman, you are essentially subtracting from the equation the role that she values most. Marketers who expect to see results in the Mom Market by lumping moms into their female communication plans will be disappointed with their results. Imagine the response you would elicit from a doctor if you omitted his or her credentials from his or her identity. After earning the title, they would almost feel insulted that you did not respect the work that went into earning the degree. Omitting the role of mom from a female with children can evoke the same emotion.

If you are an outsider looking in, we hope to give you the insights you need to establish your brand within the Mom Market and enjoy long-lasting relationships that will prevent the rush to find next month's niche du jour.

WHAT CHANGES AND
WHAT STAYS THE SAME

The Mom Market is changing, and it will continue to evolve as two new generations of mothers emerge over the next decade. If you think of marketing strategy as you would a consumer product, it's time to tweak and update your product. But in order to make the right adjustments to your marketing plan, you need to understand first what's contributing to the formation of a new generation of mothers.

Three major factors impact the change in marketing to mothers. The first is the dilution of generational influences among Baby Boomer moms. Mothers of this generation no longer function within the boundaries of generational characteristics as their predecessors did. We've found that boomer moms are less likely to act their age, instead taking on the behavior of the cohort that most resembles the moms of their children. For instance, a 45-year-old boomer mother who has a toddler is apt to behave more similarly to a Gen X mom who has a toddler than a 45-year-old mother who has a teen heading off to college. This is a critical bit of information for marketers who have been segmenting mothers by their age rather than by the ages of their children. Our research proves that the age of the child is a far more critical segmenting tool than the age of the mother.

The second factor changing the tide in marketing to moms is the growing number of tech-savvy moms as Generation Xers continue to grow their families and the Gen Y young women start theirs. These women have grown up with technology in all forms and multimedia advertising, with more options for receiving and seeking information than all previous generations combined. As mothers, they expect marketers to appeal to their multisensory communication behavior. They will challenge marketers to think well beyond the typical marketing toolbox to deliver messages in new ways that integrate their lifestyles.

Marketers today are faced with the challenge of marketing to distinct groups of women, each of whom carry their own ideas on parenting, peer influence, work and family balance, and consumer brands. This is an important piece of the puzzle that is needed to form a strong connection and build brand loyalty.

COMMON CHARACTERISTICS OF MOMS— TODAY AND TOMORROW

In the following pages we will examine the specific generational traits that influence the behavior of mothers in particular age groups. It will be especially important to understand the tendencies of the Gen X and Y moms because so many Boomers are now mimicking the behavior of their younger peers as they share the common experience of having children of the same age. Understanding the foundation on which all these groups build their values and ideas will empower us to develop effective marketing initiatives that resonate with them and grab their attention.

Before we look at the differences between mothers, it's important to recognize four common aspects of today's mothers and tomorrow's mothers-to-be.

First, you must recognize the power of mothers. This is not always easy. As a marketer today, you are faced with many decisions. At the top of the list is how to sell more products or services with fewer budgets. It's a tough challenge but a reality in companies asking us to do more with less. The good news is that marketing to moms offers a high return on investment when carried out correctly, and with the right execution can create years of brand loyalty. The bad news is that if the marketing is executed poorly or without clear goals, moms will throw out the brand with the bathwater. Hopefully, the fact that you are holding this book in your hands indicates your appreciation of the impact mothers can make on your business.

Second, you must appreciate the time mothers put into selecting a product or service. We cannot ignore the fact that moms are female shoppers with all the characteristics that go along with the title. They enjoy the experience of shopping but expect high levels of customer service. Moms want a good deal and want to be heroes to their families for saving a few extra dollars. They want selection, service, and value. Bridget Brennan of Zeno Group's Speaking Female, describes the phenomenon this way: "Women are pragmatic in their purchasing habits. The most chic woman in the neighborhood won't hesitate to brag about the $30 Isaac Mizrahi jacket she picked up at Target while doing back-to-school shopping for the kids. The new trend is for women to mix high-quality, expensive products with cheap chic. It's a shopping attitude that says, "I have great taste and enjoy high-quality products, but I'm also a shrewd buyer."

Moms also spend time researching their purchases whether online or by asking other women for their opinions. Marketers must recognize this investment of time to be successful and to determine what sets moms apart from childless females. Moms value time. Regardless if a mother has one child or eight children, all moms believe they are busy. It's the new martyrdom of motherhood. Where once mothers sacrificed their careers and personal dreams for their children, the lack of personal time in their schedules now is what mothers believe will win them their wings. Moms want retailers, service providers, and brands producers to appreciate and understand their time restraints. She wants you to live up to your brand promise so that she won't have to reinvest her initial product research time. A mother wants you to say through actions, pricing, service, and messaging, "We/this company/this brand understands you are busy and we want to help." But she doesn't want you to say it in those words. Isn't that just like a woman? She wants you to say it by sending her relevant messages that apply to her lifestyle needs and delivering on your brand promises.

Third, you must understand what it means to be a mother. Our favorite expression when speaking to clients is "You have to walk in her shoes." Marketers often assume because they know women who are moms professionally or socially, that they know the Mom Market. Others believe that because they launched a women's brand during their career, they know how mothers purchase products. Although these professionals do retain a knowledge base, they don't have the intellectual tools to successfully capture a mother's buying power. In order to win your way into a mom's wallet, marketing professionals must "walk in her shoes." What does she do between nursery school drop-off and parking at the office? Where is she going on her lunch hour and why? When does she feel most like a mom? All these are useful pieces of information that when linked together in a chain of insights will lead you to her purse.

And fourth, you must understand the generational differences that exist within today's Mom Market. Not all mothers are created equal. They are impacted by social and cultural elements; but what sets them apart from their male counterparts is the impact of their own mothers as they become mothers themselves. It's a relationship that is important to understand. A mother's relationship with her own mother lays the foundation for her values, beliefs, and ultimate buying decisions. Great historians may disagree with the passion of two niche marketers, but the relationship between mothers and daughters is a telling measure of future economics, sociological changes, and cultural trends. More importantly to marketers, it explains why moms behave the way they do as consumers. A Baby Boomer mother who grew up in a nuclear family will behave differently than the Generation X mother who was raised in a divorced household. The perception of family and marriage are quite different in these two cohorts, thus their reaction to a family-focused ad may evoke two different responses. Days of relying on "If it was good enough for my mom to use with me, then it must be good enough for me to use with my children" type of marketing are coming to an end as younger technology-savvy moms are collecting information to make their own buying decisions. Old, well-established brands will need to find new ways to attract today's moms to their mothers' favorite products.

Mothers don't always appreciate the gift they have been given. Overwhelmingly and not surprisingly, a mother's mother has or has had the greatest impact on parenting style, according to 50 percent of survey participants. A mother's own abilities are important as well, with 28 percent of survey participants reporting that they themselves have had the greatest impact on their roles and abilities as mothers. Other influences include husbands or partners, grandmothers, friends, fathers, television programs, or sisters, although none wield nearly the same weight. No significant generational differences exist among the responses. The responses were similar when we asked mothers who they most often go to as a resource for parenting advice. Significantly more Gen X and Gen Y respondents say their mothers are the one most important source for parenting advice than Boomers do.

GENERATIONALLY SPEAKING

The idea of generation gaps is not a new concept. In fact, all through history differences have been recorded between adults and their offspring. New ideas and progressive thoughts have been the core of progress. Mothers warn their children about running fast on a sidewalk, yet speed has taken us to the moon. Moms caution their toddlers about jumping from the top of a staircase, yet these daredevils discover new ways to fly. Childish ideas like pet rocks and mood rings made millions of dollars for their inventors. Understanding what moves a generation can mean increased sales for today's companies. Thankfully for marketers, authors William Strauss and Neil Howe have penned many words regarding the generational differences that exist in today's society. But never before has anyone examined the gaps that exist within the most powerful consumer market in the United States—the Mom Market. As Baby Boomer mothers begin to age, Generation X moms begin to make their mark, and Generation Y women think about having children, it is important for marketers to understand what works, what doesn't, and where the opportunity for success lies in the Mom Market. What is new about our examination of generations is the impact that mothers play on shaping the next generation of moms.

Modern sociologists who study generational groups often examine the political, economic, and social events that have shaped the feelings and views of the individuals who make up the population. Simultaneously, they agree that it is sometimes difficult to separate generational effects from other life influences to clearly define a generation. Our point of view, however, focuses on one consistency among all women of a generation, whether it is a unifying war, stock market crash, or national disaster: Every person of that generation is influenced by her mother. The relationship that a mother has with her own mother, regardless of decade of birth or generational label, clearly affects her own personal parenting style and image of herself as a mom. In other words, mothers are constantly birthing, raising, and influencing the next generation of mothers who will, in turn, continue the cycle in the future. Decade to decade the U.S. population of mothers has impacted corporate growth, political outcomes, and cultural trends. That is why we chose this as our starting point to illustrate the similarities and differences among today's mothers and to help us identify trends as tweens and teenagers become tomorrow's moms.

Marketers should keep in mind that generational variables drive different behaviors, attitudes, and choices among mothers. Second, Generation X moms respond differently to marketing efforts because of their familiarity with technology, and, finally, there is a dilution of influence among Baby Boomers that can cause them to behave more like Gen Xers than like their own cohort.

Although we will focus on the distinct differences that exist between various generations of mothers, a number of commonalities transcend the age of any mother. Moms spend money, making them a very powerful consumer group. When it's time to purchase, all moms put a great deal of time and effort into selecting the right product or service for herself or her family. However, it is not only moms who share common behavior. Ironically, marketers who want to tap the Mom Market must understand what it means to be a mother, regardless of their products, services, or target subsegments of moms.

As Baby Boomer mothers begin to age, Generation X moms begin to make their mark and Generation Y women think about having children, it is important for marketers to understand what works, what doesn't, and where the opportunity for success lies in the mom market. What is new about our examination of generations is the impact that mothers play on shaping the next generation of moms.

2

TALKING ABOUT MY GENERATION

Jennifer Murphy, a 40-year-old mother of two teenage sons in Woodland Park, Colorado, gave one of the best explanations of how mothers define generations: "I feel like I'm not really in a generation. I have a nontypical view—all my friends my age are just beginning their families. Because I had children at a young age, I feel like I'm different from them. I'm not part of Gen X or the Baby Boomers. . . . I feel like my peer group is made of women who have children the same age as mine, even though the mothers may be significantly older than me. Women my age are just starting their families." Murphy continued by saying that her disassociation with the classic notion of a generation doesn't diminish the importance of her childhood friends, but said, "If I met one of them now, we probably wouldn't have that much in common. [But we have our

Generation Y	1977–1994	57 million
Generation X	1965–1976	50 million
Baby Boomers	1946–1964	70 million
Silver Birds	1935–1945	

histories and that's what the friendship is based on.] I'm in a unique place—my oldest child is going off to college—and my husband and I are starting to look at what we're going to do and who we will become when our kids leave home. It's about life stage as an individual and that's not something others in my generation are necessarily thinking about now."

When we think about a generation, many of us rely on textbook definitions that describe a generation as the average interval of time between the birth of parents and the birth of their offspring. For many, it's a 20-year age span. While there is no definitive authority on the precise years that classify a generation, the U.S. Bureau of the Census describes Baby Boomers as people born between 1946 and 1964. Of them, approximately 40 million are mothers. Generation Xers were born between 1965 and 1976 and account for 15.6 million mothers. And Gen Y, individuals born between 1977 and 1994, adds millions more mothers to the mix with more on the way.[1]

Social scientists have concluded that noted sociologist Norman Ryder was on to something when he published a thesis in 1951 that still serves as the guiding tenet. Ryder reasoned that it is not so much an individual's age or generation that places a person in a meaningful category, but rather it is the events that occur at critical points in the lifetime of a group that creates a common bond. And so the notion of the cohort effect was born.[2]

GENERATION GAP AND GEL

We agree that the social events and influences of previous groups significantly shape the attitudes, values, and behavior of a generation. For first-wave Baby Boomers, events such as the assassination of President John F. Kennedy or the Vietnam War critically united them. Late Boomers felt the sting of the resignations of a country's vice president and then president. *Roe v.*

Wade shifted the social calculus with the legalization of abortion and the Immigration Act of 1965 paved the way for a nation that would quickly evolve into a melting pot. Gen X became firmly established as the science and technology generation with the launch of *Columbia,* America's first reusable spacecraft, in 1981, and the start of the personal computer revolution. And with President George H. W. Bush's call for a kinder, gentler nation, thousands of this generation became Points of Light, sending volunteerism and charitable contributions to an all-time high. Gen Xers experienced the significant change in the American family, with more divorces, a greater number of mother-only families, and more women seeking college and advanced degrees. The 1990s ushered in the era of electronics and the World Wide Web, and introduced a new style of communication—thumbnail. Members of the Generation Y crowd have experienced a whirlwind of social change—the Clinton impeachment proceedings, demonstrating the country's fascination with the destruction of heroes and disregard for public figures' private lives; the devastating teen-masterminded massacre at Columbine; and the turn of a new century—all juxtaposed against a booming economy and record low unemployment.[3]

Maddy Dychtwald, author of *Cycles: How We Will Live, Work, and Buy,* suggests, based on her studies of demographics, "The roles and activities we choose are much less likely to be determined by how old we are. It's not unusual to see a 35-year-old or a 65-year-old starting a new career; a 30-year-old or a 70-year-old getting married; a 45-year-old or a 25-year-old graduating from school. Age is no longer the ultimate definer of who we are, what we're doing, how we feel on the inside, what group we're a member of, or the products and services we demand from the marketplace."[4]

Major life events or milestones like Dychtwald describes, such as embarking on a new career or marriage, have a profound impact on women, influencing their lifestyle choices and their purchase decisions. But mothers are a different story. Our

decadeslong experience in the arena of marketing to moms so-
lidified our notion that moms don't fit neatly in a box with a bow.

To get our arms wrapped around this enigma, we asked
moms across the country, of various socioeconomic and demographic backgrounds, to describe their views about a generation.
We learned that their definition of a generation transcends
chronology and the typically profound impact of group experiences. In this book we segment mothers into traditional generational groups, including Baby Boomers, Generation X, and
Generation Y, because the age of a group of individuals and the
impact of cultural and societal movements does shape their attitudes and behaviors. These "generalizations," however, will
never capture the essence of individuality that all human be-
ings possess, especially mothers. As a marketer to mothers, one
can't rely solely on the chronology of a generation, but instead
one must understand the day-to-day events that impact the
women who find themselves with children of the same age and
experiencing life-stage events at the same time. For them, it's
about connecting with other mothers in their lives today, as
much as the 20-year span of people who happened to be born
at the same time and share the same cultural influences.

In talking with hundreds of mothers in one-on-one and
group settings, we learned that they tend to think about a generation as a visual family structure, the snapshot-like composite
of her grandmother, mother, herself, and her children. Many
of the moms who took part in our research described a generation with the word *grandmother* then *mom*. They described the
mental images that represented the memories, experiences,
and influences of the women who came before them. The impact of those connected, sequential relationships is apparent in
moms' parenting styles, lifestyle interests, home décor choices,
health care attitudes, and work/life preferences.

The second common way moms view a generation is interesting, too. Women don't think about generations in broad
terms but rather as the close social network they encounter on

a regular basis or even on a daily basis: friends, colleagues, neighbors, members of the PTA, or people who share the same interests, such as scrapbooking, bunko, or tennis. They believe these women are part of their generation because they share the same values and interests, but most important, because they have similarly aged children. These women mimicked Dychtwald's understanding that age has less to do with membership in a generation, but in this case, it is often the age of the children through which they view their generation.

Women are complicated as individuals, with all the emotional, intellectual, and physical trappings that come with the gender. But adding the mothering layer creates an even more complicated and complex human being. She's simultaneously defining herself through professional affiliations, hobbies, and interests, and being defined in her role as nurturer, caregiver, arbiter, coach, cook, liaison, COO, CFO, and taxi driver. She's a female who—like her thirtysomething counterparts—grew up with the lyrics of *Like a Virgin* in her ears and the innate belief that she should pay for her space on the planet through community service and volunteerism. As a classically defined Gen Xer, she may be skeptical of advertising claims, possess a strong entrepreneurial bent, and embrace technology. But consider how her role as a mom can recast her as a member of her generation.

Let's assume our Generation X woman, born in 1966, has her first child in 2005. She's 39 years old. How different is she from the Gen X woman, born in 1980, who has her first child in 2005? At the printing of this book, she's 25. In mom years, 25 to 38 is a big spread. In nonmom settings, these women might be challenged to find things in common. However, because they have a child the same age, the two are more likely to encounter each other and establish a relationship. At the playground, the tumbling class, or the preschool committee meeting, these two mothers, while technically of different generations, find their current childrearing experiences mirrored in the other, and share this bond.

The Gymboree Generation

Gymboree® Play & Music is one of the nation's leading parent/child program developers focused on the physical and psychosocial development of children. The company, founded in 1976 by a mom in California looking for an ideal environment for new parents and children to interact, has grown to become the world leader in play and music classes in 27 countries at more than 530 locations and is likely to provide some of the first structured activities for a new mom and infant. It's probably fair to assume that because the majority of women with children between the ages of newborn to five years old chronologically fall within the Generation X cohort, programs like Gymboree would consider those moms their sweet spot. We encourage you to consider a different paradigm. What if parent/child play programs revised their thinking about who they target as potential customers and defined their sweet spot as mothers of infants and toddlers, regardless of the mothers' ages? Now you have an expanded definition of a target market generation that is wider and more inclusive. Consider the power of this paradigm if you add the element of the retail store. From its roots as a play and music provider, Gymboree Corporation expanded its offering to include more than 600 children's apparel stores in the United States, Canada, the United Kingdom, and Ireland, as well as through an online store. By leveraging the target of any-age mothers with young children, you've created a potential base of mothers who represent the ripple effect, inviting peripheral consumers, such as Silver Birds, into the fold.

IMPORTANCE OF GENERATIONAL SHIFTS AMONG MOMS

"We are at the beginning chord of a generational shift," says Mark Trahant, editor of the *Seattle Post-Intelligencer*'s Editorial Page. "I know a lot of folks turning 50 this year—and I should—because some 10,000 people a day are facing a cake bearing all of those candles."[5] Social demographers and marketers are tuning in as the first wave of Baby Boomers begins to pass its generational torch to the younger Boomers, those fortysomethings bringing up the rear, who in due course will do the same to the Generation Xers behind them. The impact of this particular generational shift will be felt through the hallways and boardrooms of corporate America, in houses of worship, and in nonprofit organizations who are counting on the country's new retirees to pick up a cause instead of a paycheck. On the back lots of motion picture studios and on New York's fashion runways, another generational shift is emerging, as the hard edge of story lines and hemlines of Gen Xers gives way to the more nostalgic feel embraced by Generation Y. Finally, colleges and universities coast-to-coast are preparing for the exit of the more traditional student and the onslaught of the Gen Y generation, who represents not only a wholly new student profile, but also a wholly new profile of parent. The overprotective shield of the Baby Boomer parents will have as profound an impact on campuses nationwide as the student body itself. "Higher education leaders can identify such generational differences as the millennial generation entering college in 2000 and colliding with the Generation X students. Accounts of demanding parents, extended long-distance phone calls from families, and increasing familial interference have caused higher education leaders to examine the reemergent influence and increased expectations placed on staff members by the families of the millennial students.

Generational shifts occur among the population of mothers as well, but the nature of a generational shift with mothers and the impact of it are different. It's not surprising, given that we define generations of mothers by the age of their children, that we describe the generational shifts of moms in the same way. A moms' generational shift is not only the traditional maturing of an age group, but it is the milestones of her children that drive the exchange. Jennifer Murphy's story of a child leaving for college is one being played out in homes across the country. More than one million teens will leave for college this year, and moms are finding themselves part of a naturally occurring generational shift.[6] Jennifer Murphy is experiencing the same lifestyle decisions and identity issues as women who are typically older, so as a result of her child's milestone, she is a first-wave Baby Boomer instead of a woman who was born at the very tail end of that generational cohort. The women in this particular shift are interesting.

Consider this: As women experience the natural growth and passages of their children—from infancy to toddlerhood, from toddlerhood to preschool, from preschool to grade school, from grade school to high school, from high school to college—they enter a new "sub" generation of mother. As this happens, moms abandon some of their naiveté, relinquish their position as protégés, and assume the title of mentors. If graduating from college is seen as the passage from child to adult, the ultimate mentor is the mother whose child graduates from college. As their children grow, mothers migrate along a preordained path from uncertainty and doubt as new moms to a place where they are certain, surefooted in their experience and knowledge. And they pass this wisdom on to the mothers who follow, nurturing a new generation of protégé mothers, along the way influencing attitudes, lifestyle choices, and especially purchase decisions. The profound impact these mothers have on their Gen X successors as well as the generation that preceded them is significant. But there's a flip side, too. The boomer mother is often influenced—and inspired—by the Gen X mom, especially if they have children the same age.

Ellen Wessel is president of Moving Comfort, a Virginia-based sports apparel company focused solely on women. "We see the influence one group of mothers has on another in lots of ways. Many mothers we talk to tell us they remember what they looked like and felt like before they had kids, and many of them aspire to look and feel like that again," said Wessel, who went on to explain that in an organized sports group, such as the Atlanta Lawn Tennis Association or a running club, or even classes at a neighborhood gym, Gen X mothers may influence boomer mothers who are newly committing to or reigniting a fitness regimen. Boomer moms may look to the Gen Xers for advice on workout routines and head-to-toe apparel, seeking recommendations on everything from running shoe models and sports bras to retailers who offer the best-fit advice and customer service. In turn, the boomer mothers will share with them what to expect in terms of their changing bodies, pediatricians, and even educational options for their kids.

Clearly, the influence of these generations of moms runs from older to younger and vice versa, and can be felt in retail establishments, restaurants, playgrounds, and schools across the country. Robin Lattizzori, principal at Mount Bethel Elementary School in Marietta, Georgia, described the influence of different generations of moms by saying, "In a school environment, there's a natural progression in the growth and experience levels of mothers. The mother of a kindergarten student is almost certainly a different mother when her child completes fifth grade. She walked in unsure about what to do, and by the end, she's running the PTA."

As generations shift, another interesting thing happens. A race begins, in which a jockeying of position between the roles of mother and woman occurs. A new mom, regardless of age, consumed with the experience of caring for a newborn and adjusting to this major life change is a mother first and foremost. As her child ages, she begins to reconnect with her nonmom side, perhaps taking up a hobby or activity that she temporarily abandoned, volunteering, or reentering the workforce. This scenario is easy to imagine when thinking about mothers whose children are entering their late teen years, regardless of whether mom is 40 or 50. As part of the natural life course, she begins to significantly transition her role from primarily "mom" to a newly envisioned version of herself. She's far from becoming obsolete as a mom, but her children's growing independence and movement toward adulthood enable her to focus more on redefining herself and her role as a mother—one that allows her to renew her identity. Unforgedibles, a gourmet café and take-out service in the suburbs of Atlanta, was the brainchild of Laura Taylor, Laurie Wicker, Deborah Ruskin, and Dawn Scott, who range in age from 43 to 49. The four friends described how they awoke to the fact that they were no longer the mothers of children who urgently needed them, but mothers of teenagers who were independent and occupied with a full slate of activities—many that did not include the moms. In describing why they opened the restaurant, Laura Taylor explained, "I never finished college. Now my son is 15 and my daughter is 13 and I don't want them to know me only as a stay-at-home mom. I wanted to show them I could be more than that." Partner Deborah Ruskin wanted to create something that was hers, a place where she could give in to her passion for food and entertaining. "We want to make an impact on the next generation," added Laurie Wicker. "My grandfather had the only nonunion steel mill in Ohio. I worked on the line beginning when I was eight years old. He should have left it to me, but he had only girls in the family, and he believed girls weren't up to running a business like that." The friends described how they were influenced by the legacy of their mothers, which made it important to send a strong message to their daughters. Aside from their kitchen shenanigans, what makes these women interesting is that the foursome originally became friends as a result of neighborhood connections and the kid-focused activities they all supported as a result of their children. In time, two of the friends strengthened their connection by working together in a catering business and, as they say, the rest is history, a history these women are glad to have together.

Mayfield Dairies understands the importance of the generational shift between mothering groups and the resulting influence that occurs between them as the baton is being passed. "We have a better chance of getting a young mother to become our customer in a market where her mom served Mayfield," says Mayfield Dairies President Scottie Mayfield. "There's an attitude that milk is milk, so it comes down to price. But we don't view milk as milk and we do some things that most other dairies don't do. Kids grow up with the taste of Mayfield. As they grow up, they may have abandoned milk, but then they have kids and they want their kids to have milk, so they turn to us."

GETTING IT DONE

There is one thing, though, that every mother wants regardless of her generational label. She wants to be productive. She wants to be able to get traction, to accomplish something meaningful. If you ask a mother, or any woman for that matter, how she defines a good day, chances are she'll tell you it's when she's able to get things done, whether successfully getting to all her errands or completing a long-standing project. It's about accomplishment, and to a mother, who constantly lives her life juggling the needs and demands of family and friends, the opportunity to accomplish is meaningful. For mothers, productivity takes on an added element of importance. Being productive means creating something, a building block or stepping-stone that helps provide purpose for the next day's activities. This might be working to potty-train a toddler or getting laundry done early so she can curl up with a good book before bedtime. According to Atlanta psychologist Robert D. Simmermon, it's a challenge for mothers to move their children or families forward without productivity and as a result, they can't progress to the next stage in their own lives, be it day-to-day, year-to-year, or generation-to-generation.

Mothers appreciate companies and brands that help facilitate their need for productivity. Years ago when pay-at-the-pump gas stations became readily available, moms cheered from coast-to-coast. One of moms' biggest frustrations—especially during the car seat years—is getting kids in and out of a car to pay for goods and services. Imagine the cheer that went up when moms no longer had to choose whether to dash for the cashier in the store with the kids in the car or go through the aggravation of taking young kids out of the car and into the store. The gas stations obtained rock star status overnight as a result of this seemingly simple technological advancement. And moms anywhere will tell you they'll bypass a service station that doesn't offer pay-at-pump convenience, even if it's more convenient.

Procter & Gamble's Swiffer hard-surface floor-cleaning system was introduced in 1999 and only a few years later is one of the products most frequently mentioned in our interviews with mothers as a product or brand that most makes life easier. Moms really aren't hard to please; just give them a broom-and-mop combination that significantly cuts the cleaning time and reduces mess, and they're happy. *Mass Market Retailers,* a trade publication for the supermarket, drug, and discount chain stores, referred to the Swiffer Wet Jet as a megahit. And the hits keep coming as new extensions to the Swiffer lineup make their way off store shelves and into moms' pantries.[7]

It's a common mistake, though, to confuse a mother's need for productivity with convenience or choice. We believe convenience and choice are logical outcomes of productivity. For example, in the frozen-food aisle of a typical suburban supermarket, one can find at least 12 brands of ice cream, yogurts, and sorbets, and 43 subbrands, in all representing more than 300 flavor variations. That's choice, but is it convenience? It requires emotional, physical, and intellectual energy to make choices. Once a choice is made, consumers mentally defend their choice to ensure they've gotten the best value and paid the right amount of money for that value. Thus, consumers must be informed, which means doing their homework, which means more work and more energy devoted to choosing a quart of ice cream.

Mothers have precious little energy to spare so the key is to make their choice easy and convenient, and, overall, productive.

RITUALS

Think about the first three things you do when you wake up in the morning. Over the years, we've asked thousands of mothers this question and we tend to get the same sets of answers each time. It's not surprising that they answer "Turn off the alarm clock," "Get my glasses," "Go to the bathroom," or "Turn on the coffeepot." It's not the answers that are important or profound. What is important is the notion that we all have rituals. Rituals provide a framework for how we interact with the world around us. All mothers have rituals and successful marketers understand that it's easier to insinuate a product or service into a mom's existing routine than it is to ask her to change or even add a new routine to her agenda. Any number of commercial and not-for-profit entities has successfully incorporated their offerings into moms' routines. The YMCA network made it easier for mothers to maintain their workout rituals with onsite childcare and babysitting. Starbucks enabled moms to enjoy their morning caffeine by offering a series of child-friendly drinks and juices. And savvy supermarket operators recognized that a grocery cart designed to look like a race car could make the ritual of food shopping that much easier when mom brings the kids along.

TRADITION, NOSTALGIA, AND INTERGENERATIONAL RELATIONSHIPS

Mothers didn't start out as mothers. They started out as daughters. And over two or three or even four decades, the values, parenting style, and traditions of their own mothers shaped the way they make purchasing decisions. High-profile retailers, such as Gap stores, have tapped into the importance of inter-generational connectivity. Iconic retailer Gap tapped into the popularity of generational connectivity with an interesting campaign that aired in the fall of 2002 entitled "For Every Generation." In one of the spots, rock icon Marianne Faithful, Taryn Manning, and new R&B star Tweet wear Long and Lean jeans while delivering a new spin to the Staple Singers classic song, *I'll Take You There.* Birkenstock, a leading brand of comfort shoes, is attempting to bridge the generations with a new marketing campaign and product grouping that targets a 25- to 35-year-old customer. A Birkenstock representative described the company's approach by explaining that the product lines are more about a shopper's lifestyle than about age.[8]

What marketers need to know about using tradition in advertising or communications is that it's about chemistry. Tradition is composed of four equal parts: consistency, repetition, endurance, and stability. According to Simmermon, a tradition can take hold only if it has consistent parameters. A holiday, for example, is typically celebrated the same time each year or during the same season each year. The holiday rituals are repeated in the same manner and follow prescribed steps each year, such as lighting candles and telling stories. This celebration has an established history and a future that is typically passed on to subsequent generations, which is endurance. This holiday is widely accepted and not subject to change or alteration on a regular basis. What mothers commonly do, though, is modify traditions to suit their particular lifestyles, life stages, and needs, creating in essence their "new" traditions.

The pull towards nostalgia can be seen everywhere, from vintage clothing stores and the reemergence of licensed characters, such as Superman or Strawberry Shortcake, to nostalgic candy stores and movie themes. Nostalgia and tradition are kissing cousins; we yearn for the good memories and grounding that nostalgia delivers, and traditions can be the route to nostalgia. Mothers' unquenchable thirst for nostalgia can even be found on grocery store shelves. Nothing churns up nostalgic memories and the emotional pull for "the good old days" like a holiday mealtime. It's easy to conjure up images of mom spending hours preparing and cooking a holiday turkey or beef roast. A mother today can attach to those memories and continue a family tradition on her terms without having to dedicate six hours to cooking a turkey. Today, companies such as Reynolds are catering to moms' desire for nutritious but quickly prepared meals with products like Oven Bags, allowing them to satisfy their ritual of cooking with a new tradition of doing so.

Lisa Stone, founder and CEO of Fit For 2, a high-energy-group fitness program for pregnant women and mothers with new babies, and mother of three, offered her own definitions of generations of moms. "In the textbook sense, I think of a generation of mothers in terms of age, but from a marketing perspective, and with mothers in particular, you can't just look at the age of the mothers, but the ages of the kids. The first generation of moms is those who are pregnant. They're really a group unto themselves. We should really be more specific and include a subgroup of women pregnant with their first child. They are very hungry for knowledge and are also very self-focused. The ability to appeal to them from the angle about establishing motherhood and designing what motherhood is going to look like from their perspective is important for marketing purposes." Lisa continued by describing the second group, which encompassed mothers who are pregnant with subsequent children. Marketing to them becomes more about convenience and ease and time management. "A panic can set in when you have a child, children, and an infant on the way." The third group is mothers with babies. This group of women is dealing with sleep deprivation, energy deprivation, romance deprivation, and privacy deprivation. Stone advises marketers to attend to those types of issues with messages about how their lives can be made easier. "It's so important to remember that if a mom has multiple children and a baby, always market to the youngest common denominator. It's most often about the baby," Stone added. The next group is mothers of school-age children. When the children enter school, mothers finally have breathing room. While the kids are in school, mothers don't have to provide 100 percent focus as they do with a child at home. Moms of elementary schoolers are eager for school to be in session because they need a break from the constant demands of a summer schedule. On the other hand, moms of older kids prefer summer because of the homework, school activities, class, and extracurricular projects, and transportation drain. Stone describes the final group as mothers of middle-school children primarily because of the intensity of the schoolwork and the planning that mothers have to do to ensure homework assignments are completed, errands are run, dinner is cooked, and the household is running. These mothers are looking for convenience, too, but Stone cautions that it's couched in a need for simplification.

Before we examine the generational traits of today's mothers, it's important to understand the changing roles of a mother within her family and how it impacted her relationship with her children, some of whom make up today's Mom Market. No other lifestyle element has changed her role more than her return to the workforce. The 1960s saw mothers leaving the kitchen and entering the halls of corporate America in record numbers. This steady stream of career-minded mothers affected many areas of American life. Suddenly, mothers were spending less time with their children, which subsequently impacted the future generation of mothers. It also reconfigured the shape of the American family, established the lucrative Mom Market, and bred emotions that led to changed values and priorities for American mothers forever. Let's take a look at how work has defined the role of mothers throughout the generations.

3

WORKING IT
Mothers in the Office

Every morning in America, two out of three mothers with children under 5 years of age leave the house for the workplace.[1] According to the U.S. Department of Labor, 72 percent of mothers with children under 18 are in the workforce.[2] The staggering number makes it difficult to believe that there ever was a generation of mothers who did not populate our workforce. But if you consider that women, whether with child or without, have only had the right to vote since 1920, it's not surprising that the career of working mothers is short in terms of America's history. The old Virginia Slims' slogan, "You've come a long way, baby," can certainly apply to the progress and growth mothers have had in corporate America. In fact, if you consider that a third of working women earn more than their spouses do, you'll fully appreciate how far women have traveled in their careers. Life as a mother has changed since the days when Baby Boomers where children. Their mothers, known as the Silent Generation, spent their days in the home caring for the children and doing household chores. Baby Boomers grew up in an era when young people challenged the established institutions. Together with the birth of the women's lib movement, Baby Boomer women entered the workplace even after having children.

We asked mothers to describe each of the four traditional generations of mothers and we found it noteworthy that the adjectives used were so varied among each grouping. Moreover, each generation is more likely to assign positive attributes to themselves and less flattering attributes to other generations. For example, more Baby Boomer mothers describe themselves as hardworking than do Generation X moms. More Generation X and Generation Y moms label themselves as strong as do Baby Boomers and Silver Birds. To put this in context, Baby Boomer moms view themselves as hardworking (76 percent), strong (74 percent), competitive (62 percent), confident (61 percent), and driven (58 percent). Gen X mothers are more inclined than other generations to describe Baby Boomer mothers as conservative and following the pack.

The entry of mothers into the workforce set off a chain of events that continues to impact almost every aspect of American life. The ability to earn a paycheck gave women with children a sense of independence and confidence that impacted the makeup of today's families. Suddenly, a woman did not need to remain married to ensure financial security for her and her children. In fact, the divorce rate in America has risen every year since 1960 and continues today.[3] According to the 2000 census, single mothers are the fastest-growing demographic in the United States, a number compounded by Gen X moms choosing to remain single rather than marry.[4]

To prepare for future uncertainties, the children of boomer moms turned their focus to education. In the eyes of Generation Xers, education is the key to controlling one's own destiny, the essence of personal security. The result is that this new generation of women is better equipped than ever to be the breadwinner of the family. Women are currently earning more degrees and MBAs than are men. In 2001, women held almost half of all high-paying "executive, administrative, and managerial occupations."[5] But unlike their mothers, Generation Xers came to the workplace on their terms. They didn't see their first employer as a long-term partner but rather as a training ground for more education. Along with their briefcases they also carried their skepticism with them. They had watched their mothers blaze the trails in work and family balance and with their experiences as children etched in their minds, they demanded the options that enable them to be a mother and an employee. When they were not happy with their experience working within corporate America, they did what they knew best, they found their own solution. Many applied their knowledge of technology and the survivor skills learned as self-sufficient kids to business and started their own companies. Today, women are starting businesses at four times the rate of men.[6] The term *momprenuer* is widely recognized.

Our quick lesson in history now brings us to the present. According to the Bureau of the Census, the number of working mothers age 15 to 44 with infants under 1 year, dropped to 55 percent from 59 percent in 1998. This was the first decline since the bureau started keeping track in 1976.[7] This might initially have sparked the conclusion that moms were returning to the role of June Cleaver, staying home to be full-time mothers. But don't be deceived. A mass exodus of mothers from the workplace was not on our horizon. In fact, quite the contrary, the impact of mothers in the workplace will continue to grow; it will just be on new terms using new terms.

REDEFINING BALANCE

Many hypotheses exist about the decline in the number of working mothers. We prefer to isolate the number as a snapshot of just one moment in a long span of history and events to come. This approach is important in supporting our hypothesis and considering other possibilities. First, let's examine the thinking of others about the overall decline in working mothers. Some say that the turn occurred in response to September 11, when the security of our nation was rocked. Americans took a harder look at their own priorities and values and made decisions based on their newfound emphasis on family security and concerns about decreased workplace security. Some psychologists claim that mothers believed it was more important to stay at home rather than return to the workplace. And the prosperity of the Internet enabled more mothers to relinquish the need for a second income and remain in the home. Although both likely contribute in some way to the decisions of mothers, we tend to believe the answer is found in the generational differences of Boomers and Generation Xers and the words they used to describe the experience of work.

To begin to understand these differences, you need to go only as far as the term, *working mother.* To Boomers this meant getting up every morning, packing up the children, making a stop at daycare, and rushing off to the office. Working mother meant traveling to an office outside the home. This experience forced mothers to become master multitaskers not only with their daily chores but with their emotions as well. They struggled between enjoying their newfound careers, pushing themselves to their personal limits, and managing their inherent nature to nurture their children. Guilt emerged as a unifying emotion and served as the catalyst for boomer working mothers to find balance in their lives, rather than wanting to do it all. In our research, phrases such as "I learned I can do anything" were juxtaposed with "It all just got jumbled together." One of our favorite phrases that describes a mom's life that is balanced between work and nonwork activities is, "This is the ideal life that takes patience and mistakes to achieve. This life must be flexible and willing to constantly change."

For retailers, the quest for balance spawned new categories of products such as massages, whirlpool tubs, and scented candles. It also offered marketers the opportunity to present new messaging that provided solutions to everyday challenges. A new wave of service providers and destinations clamored to provide a balanced life to these overworked mothers with spa retreats and self-help classes. The boomer definition of a working mother meant finding a balance between being a mother and working outside the home. Many have learned it's a delicate balance difficult to obtain and even harder to maintain. Baby Boomers didn't learn this lesson alone, however, for their daughters were looking over their shoulders.

The children of Baby Boomers watched silently as their mothers struggled to keep this delicate balance between work and family. As outside observers, they were able to apply their own objectivity and independent thinking to the situation. They concluded that balance could not be easily obtained and could lead to more insecurity in life. In their constant quest for the family security they missed as a child, they decided not to approach the balancing act in the same way. Instead, Generation Xers believe a mother can have it all but at different stages of her life. They replaced the idea of a balanced life with the concept of an integrated life. We see this as a movement that is about to hit the mainstream but is not yet reflected in the media or over watercooler chats. Those conversations still focus on a mother achieving work and family balance. When we spoke to mothers directly on the subject through our research, the work and family balance issue was not so great a priority as it was for prior generations. This factor was not mentioned as one of the top five traits that make a great mom; however, Gen X and Gen Y moms did say that the ability to stay home with children was an important trait (34 percent and 32 percent, respectively). After watching their parents' marriages falter or crumble under the strain of balancing work and family, they want a close family but know that at some point they might have to be the sole or primary breadwinner. They still want it all, but wisely decide not at the same time! The integrated lifestyle leaves room for the uncertainties of life with careers that no longer require being out of the home five days a week, and work that can incorporate, rather than exclude, the notion of family.

Generation Xers have utilized technology to build successful home-based businesses. Julie Aigner Clarke, founder of the Baby Einstein Videos company, applied her talents as a teacher when she began producing educational videos for children while home raising her children. Her basement became home to a multimillion-dollar business that she eventually sold to Disney. Today Clarke is launching her second business, The Safe Side, because she enjoys the entrepreneurial spirit of a Gen Xer. Home-based businesses are on the rise, offering mothers another option for attaining balance regardless of their individual definition of the term. One of every 11 women in the United States is now a business owner, according to the Center for Women's Business Research.[8] And although no one tracks the percentage of those women who are also mothers, simple math can help us estimate that the number is somewhere around 6.5 million. Gen Xers have also used technology to integrate work into their role as a mother by telecommuting, and no longer feel constrained by geography in accomplishing goals. Networks of home-based working mothers have proliferated online, and mothers collaborate with others across the country on projects such as producing children's books or designing Web sites.

Corporate America has done poorly in earning the trust of this already skeptical generation. Companies have begun cutting back on the family-friendly benefits their mothers fought so long and hard for. Paid family leave has dropped, from 27 percent in 2001 to 23 percent in 2002, according to a Society of Human Resource Management survey. While companies are offering less, working mothers are expected to do more. In a CareerBuilder .com online survey of working mothers, 36 percent said they worked more than 40 hours a week and 71 percent said their careers suffered because they chose flexible schedules. So, as their generation has done throughout their lifetime, Generation Xers have forged their own path, creating their own secure environment for achieving personal and professional fulfillment. And for many, this has meant leaving the workplace on their terms.

All this brings us back to our hypothesis on the decline in recorded number of working mothers. We believe there is less of a decline than a shift in perceptions of work. We tend to believe that researchers are asking the same question to all generations of mothers expecting to get one clear answer. If you ask a Baby Boomer mother whether she's a working mom or a stay-at-home mom, she is likely to interpret that as a self-identity or economic question. If you ask the same question of a Gen X or Gen Y mom, she is more inclined to consider that a question about her values or priorities. This is a vitally important consideration for marketing professionals who may be working to build relationships with mothers based on their need for work/home balance or business-oriented products or services. A Generation X mom may say that she is a stay-at-home mother but actually operates a lucrative eBay business from her home at night. Within her integrated lifestyle structure, she is a mom all day, enabling her to be in that role full-time, and therefore she gives it more weight than she does her professional activities.

The changing work attitudes of mothers are actually good news for marketers. For those who fully understand the new working mother, the opportunities to create product extensions and increase sales and brand loyalty come through two channels, moms as employees and moms as owners or purchasing agents for companies.

MARKETING TO MOTHERS AS EMPLOYEES

A book on marketing to mothers could not exclude a discussion on marketing to moms as employees for two very important reasons. First, moms represent a large talent pool of prospective skilled employees. Particularly as employers seek technology-savvy staff, their best prospects will be found in the Gen X and Y populations, many of whom will be mothers. Second, moms expect the companies they patronize to be sensitive to the needs of working mothers. This means you must position your company as one that attracts and retains mothers as employees. Moms expect companies to walk the talk, particularly if on the consumer side of the business they profess to serve mothers. They want you to demonstrate that you also serve them as an employer. The new generation of mothers will place more emphasis on this element because it shows the "real" side of the company. Companies who ignore this aspect of marketing to moms face a danger that mothers will recognize inconsistencies in their marketing. You also put yourself at risk on that one day the media reveals that only 20 percent of your workforce is women, although you tout being a company who believes in women. It's just not a good business decision.

The benefits gained by carrying your marketing plan all the way through to your human resources department are far greater than the effort it takes to execute it. Just look at the reputation that Avon has enjoyed as one of the top employers for workingwomen. In fact, Avon Products was named the top Fortune 1000 company of 2001 by the National Association of Female Executives on its annual list of "Top 25 Companies for Female Executives." Not only does Avon have a female chairwoman and CEO in Andrea Jung, but also, according to company information, Avon has more women in management positions (86 percent) than any other Fortune 500 company, and half of its Board of Directors are female. Avon has built its company on the strength of a female sales force, many of whom are mothers looking for a way to supplement their household incomes. Avon sends a clear message to female consumers that it supports women by producing quality products, cares about women as individuals by supporting causes such as breast cancer research, and values them as employees.

Johnson & Johnson is another company that has success-fully integrated its brand messages into the corporate culture. It was named to the top slot of *Working Mother* magazine's 2001 list of "100 Best Companies for Working Mothers." The John-son & Johnson credo outlines its responsibilities as a corpora-tion to the interests of its customers, its employees, and the communities in which they live and work. Johnson & Johnson fulfills that promise not only by providing quality products but also through programs such as the Women's Museum built in Dallas, Texas, and offering working parents work/life bene-fits that allow them to balance their work and family needs. In addition, the company supports innovative programs that serve both the needs of female employees and career-minded women as well. Recently, Johnson & Johnson pledged $20 mil-lion for a drive to recruit nurses, which is a shrinking profes-sion, to demonstrate its commitment to the cause. Television commercials as well as scholarship programs supported the event, called "Campaign for Nursing's Future." This is a good example of a community relation initiative that is consistent with the brand strategy and marketing plan of the company. It is a strategy that works because, as we have already learned, mothers want to know that the companies they are supporting are also supporting their families. In fact, according to a 1999 report released by the National Foundation for Women Busi-ness Owners (NFWBO), one in five workingwomen agrees that the social responsibility of the company offering the product or service is a major influence in her buying decision. The help mothers seek is in making their communities better for their children and in finding solutions for them as mothers. Johnson & Johnson does that by donating resources to the communities of their consumers and by offering positive employment solu-tions to working mothers. And whether a mother is actually touched by a program doesn't matter, the effect is similar to ad-vertising; she only needs to picture herself in it to believe it's there for her.

Marketing to moms as employees also increases your talent pool. By offering mom-friendly benefits such as telecommuting, flexible work schedules, or job sharing, your company will be able to retain experienced employees who might otherwise leave the workplace after giving birth. According to U.S. Department of Labor estimates, the base cost of replacing a worker is 30 percent of that person's annual earnings.[9] Gen X and Gen Y mothers who strive for an integrated rather than a balanced lifestyle will leave the workplace because of the inability to find suitable daycare, a disproportionate relationship between pay and expenses related to going to work, or managing the demands of their children. By offering flexible work schedules, daycare solutions, or other work and family balance benefits, you will be able to reduce your turnover rate and save the costs associated with replacing employees. NationsBank (now Bank of America) found that offering a $25-a-week childcare subsidy brought turnover down from 46 percent to 14 percent. These working mother–friendly benefits will become more important as Gen X and Gen Y women grow in numbers in the workplace. In fact, companies eager to fill some types of positions may not have a choice in implementing such programs if they want to recruit Gen X and Gen Y mothers.

Lynn Hennighausen, President of A Balancing Act, Inc., and author of *Shades of Gray: A Mother's Guide to Work and Family Choices* (Beaver's Pond Press, 2002), describes this trend: "Generation Xers and Gen Ys expect more flexibility—partly because women before blazed the trail, partly as a result of the economy and the values these generations represent. The downturn of the economy and the downsized workplace forced Gen Xers to take on a sort of 'free agent' role. They lack the loyalty of their parents because the workplace lacks loyalty to them. These groups saw what their parents went through and became adamant about balancing work and family."

Hennighausen points to the numbers to illustrate her point: "Twenty-eight percent of Gen X women and 28.7 percent of

Gen X men had flexible schedules in 2000, reported the Bureau of Labor Statistics. Young moms expect flexibility because it makes work, well—work well."

You don't have to earn a spot on top of *Working Mother*'s list to successfully market yourself to mothers. Your company will be able to retain mothers as employees by offering work and family benefits they value and by offering them solutions. In order to determine what benefits matter most to working mothers, view them as you would a customer and apply the same methods of marketing to consumers. Research your market, determine the need, offer a product, and market it. Begin by asking the customer what she wants and needs. Is it flexible work hours or concierge services that motivate your working mothers? Is it job sharing or childcare reimbursement? Not only will your employees appreciate your interest in their opinion but you are likely to identify employment needs that are unique to your business. It might even surprise you that some are quite inexpensive to implement. I remember hearing of a company where the working mothers' only request was a couch in the restroom so that they could sit and use a breast pump comfortably. The request was simply met the same day by moving a sofa from a departed executive's office into the ladies' lounge. The result was renewed employee morale, which translated into increased productivity. We polled working mothers on http://www.BlueSuitMom.com about the work/life benefit they valued most. More than half of the 794 respondents said flexible work hours was the most important benefit an employer can offer, with 35 percent saying on-site childcare was the most important benefit. Recent studies show employers are beginning to recognize that many of their employees would like flexibility in choosing the hours they work. The percentage of workers taking advantage of flexible hours has more than doubled since 1985, the first year the Bureau of Labor Statistics started collecting the data. Telecommuting is also becoming a popular benefit, with more than 6.5 million Americans (not including

Creative Work/Life Benefits a Company
Might Consider Offering Moms

Take-home dinners	College entrance services for
Dry-cleaning services	parents of teens
School holiday programs	"Concierge" services
On-site salon for manicures and	On-site health clubs
hair services	Tuition reimbursement
Lunch-and-learn series to offer	Eldercare programs
parenting advice	College savings plans
Financial consulting	Adoption assistance
Personal coaching	

the self-employed) telecommuting during the week.[10] To remain competitive, it is necessary to offer attractive compensation packages but also benefits that mothers value. A study by the Radcliffe Public Policy Center found that 61 percent of Americans would be willing to take a pay cut if it meant more time with their children or other family members.[11]

Working mothers represent a large, valuable pool of skill and talent that may currently be a part of your workforce or potential employees whose skills could bring yet unknown improvements to your bottom line. It is far more cost-effective to retain a valuable employee than to incur the cost of recruiting and training a new one.

MARKETING TO WORKING MOTHERS AS CONSUMERS

Few consumer product companies or service providers take full advantage of the buying power of the Mom Market because they fail to recognize a mother in her role as an employee or business owner. Even the most successful marketers will stop short of tapping into the other wallet many mothers manage, that of her employer or, increasingly, the checkbook of her own company. After the lunch boxes are packed, the groceries are bought, and the car is fueled, moms are buying computers, leasing copiers, ordering books, and requesting shipments of supplies from all over the world. In their roles as managers, contractors, service providers, manufacturers, and business owners, moms are driving a large part of the American economy. A lot of money is on the table for those companies that include marketing to moms as employees or business owners in their plan. Each day, more than 25 million mothers work, in addition to performing their duties as a mother, wife, or homemaker.[12] Mothers are taking on roles as teachers, sales professionals, office administrators, doctors, lawyers, and truck drivers. Mothers go to work in governors' mansions, penthouse CEO offices, classrooms, television studios, and on the Senate floor, and in each of these roles they are spending money. This is good news for companies who recognize moms' purchasing power beyond the home and focus on their multiple roles as moms and businesswomen. Eighty-six percent of women business owners use the same products at home that they purchase for their companies, according to the NFWBO.[13] This means two channels of consumption are available for brands that win the loyalty of a working mother. Brands such as Office Depot, Dell, Best Buy, and American Express are well poised to gain the spending of mothers controlling the wallet at home and at the office, regardless of where that office is located.

We believe the number of mom-owned businesses will continue to grow as technology-savvy Xers and Ys find ways to integrate work into their family lives. This means that while they are purchasing ink for their home printer, they will also be buying paper for their business letterhead. What marketing professional can argue with tapping two wallets with one customer? That's a good return on investment. We believe this is one of the greatest opportunities for companies in the Mom Market—to capture the untapped niche market of moms as business owners. Few people fully appreciate the magnitude of female-owned businesses in the United States. The numbers certainly speak for themselves.

So where do companies that decide to target mother business owners go to find them, especially if they are working from their homes? The Internet joins a large number of them where they find places to compare notes, get advice, and pool resources. It is easy to find pockets of these moms on sites such as Home-Based Working Mothers, http://www.hbwm.com, and Work at Home Moms, http://www.wahm.com. With even a limited marketing budget, it is possible to communicate your message to these mothers through banners, channel sponsorships, and electronic newsletter ads. When positioning your company with this niche, it is best to focus on messages that offer solutions for running their businesses more efficiently. It is important to recognize the unique challenges these mothers face in keeping their businesses separate from their families, even though both are located in their homes. Office Depot recently ran an ad that hit the bull's-eye with home-based working-women. The ad pictured a woman in her home office with this copy: "It's not a corner office with a view of the city. But it's where you do your best work. That's why your home office has to be special. From office furnishings to the latest technology, Office Depot is the expert source to provide you with what you need when you need it." The ad speaks straight to the pride a woman takes in her surroundings, her talents as a professional, and the convenience women appreciate and need.

Some marketing ideas that serve all mom business owners regardless of where their offices are located can be executed inexpensively. We suggest to clients who want to tap this market that they sponsor networking events. Women business owners like to compare ideas and like to be recognized as "real" busi-

Facts about Women in Business from the Center for Women's Business Research

- As of 2002, there were an estimated 6.2 million majority-owned, privately held women-owned firms in the United States, accounting for 28 percent of all privately held firms in the country.
- Women-owned firms in the United States employ 9.2 million people and generate $1.15 trillion in sales.
- In the past five years, the number of women-owned firms increased by 14 percent nationwide, sales grew by 40 percent, and employment increased by 30 percent.
- The number of women-owned firms increased at twice the rate of all firms (14 percent versus 7 percent), employment grew at one and a half times the rate (30 percent versus 18 percent), and revenues increased at the same rate.
- As of 2002, there were 112,712 women-owned firms with revenues of $1 million or more and 8,480 with 100 or more employees in the United States.
- The largest share of women-owned firms is in the service sector. Fifty-three percent of women-owned businesses are in services, 16 percent are in retail trade, and 9 percent are in finance, insurance, or real estate. Twelve percent are in unclassified industries.
- Women are diversifying into nontraditional industries. The greatest growth in the number of women-owned firms during the 1997 to 2002 period has been in construction, with 36 percent growth, and in agricultural services, with 27 percent growth.
- The ten states with the largest number of women-owned firms based on the average of number of firms, employment, and sales are (in descending order): California; Texas; Florida, Illinois, and New York (tied); Ohio; Michigan and Pennsylvania (tied); North Carolina; and New Jersey.

nesses. Hosting some type of mixer or educational program accomplishes both of these objectives. A bank, for instance, might host an after-hours happy hour with a short program entitled, "Obtaining Small Business Loans for Expanding Your Company." The program lets the audience know that the bank recognizes the potential of women-owned businesses and gives them a chance to network. If special event planning is not your forte, you might want to contact a local chapter of the NFWBO or the National Association of Female Executives (NAFE) and sponsor a meeting. In addition, you may want to consider print advertising in local niche publications such as business dailies or parenting newspapers.

Incorporating a marketing plan to connect with mothers as employees and business owners can present many opportunities to your company. Not only will your plan help you tap into the billions of dollars being spent by working mothers from their offices, but it also will help you retain the best employees, reduce the cost of turnover, increase productivity, boost employee morale, strengthen your consumer image, and create avenues for expansion. You only need to recognize the potential of the market, find the right message, and integrate it throughout your entire company.

Now that we understand the changing roles of mothers, it's time to see how their position has translated into generational behavior. Within the following chapters, we will take an extensive look at each generation of mothers: Baby Boomers, Generation Xers, and Generation Ys. We will even take a glimpse at what we call Silver Birds, those grandmothers who are raising grandchildren. Understanding the influences unique to their generation will enable you to develop marketing strategies that successfully tap the trillions of dollars moms are spending at the office and at home.

4

BABY BOOMERS
Parenting Pioneers

Sal Kibler grew up in the South Carolina low country, where traditions were rich and plentiful and the roles of women were understood. Now living in Atlanta, Georgia, the 50-year-old advertising agency president recalls fondly how her mother declined to accept the status quo and recast herself as a successful entrepreneur. "Mom owned her own business, so she tried to manage situations, home and work. She created a work situation that allowed her to do that. She pushed me into the world and made me experience things, like the social and academic worlds," Kibler explained. "I learned to manage my life without much management from her. I find parents today take on a lot more responsibility for their kids . . . certainly more than my mother did with me. As a result, I grew up more independent and I hope the same for my children." These gutsy females, like Kibler's mother, started a movement that took root with the boomer generation and fostered the era of the working mother.

To truly understand the values, work, and home lifestyles and preferences of Baby Boomer mothers, we have to consider where they came from and who influenced them. A lot has been written about the profound impact that Baby Boomer mothers had on their children as a result of the mass migration into the workforce. But less has been written about the generation of women who raised the boomer moms and established a platform for one of the most influential cohorts in history. The women we call Silver Birds are critically important in mothering society today, not only for their influence on their Baby Boomer daughters, but because many of them are raising or serving as primary caregivers for their grandchildren. We talk more in-depth about the impact of these Silver Birds on the educational status, lifestyle decisions, and care and feeding of their grandchildren later in the book. For this chapter, however, let's consider the cultural climate and economic conditions in the years between 1935 and 1945.

SILVER BIRDS IN AND OUT OF THE NEST

The women of the World War II generation matured wearing the stain of the Great Depression. They became self-sufficient and dependent simultaneously, devising ingenious ways to entertain themselves and capitalizing on government programs such as the Public Works of Art project and other federal public works initiatives. This was a time when families looked ahead to their next meal, not to their next vacation. It was an era when women such as Mildred "Babe" Didrikson and Wilma Rudolph (two of America's finest female athletes), Amelia Earhart (an aviation pioneer and the first woman to fly solo across the Atlantic Ocean), and Frances Perkins (the first female cabinet member who advocated the eight-hour workday and the enactment of laws for the protection of women and children in the labor force) helped shape a new aspirational identity for other women, expanding the possibilities of what being female could mean in America during the 1930s. The image of Rosie the Riveter may best exemplify the collective potential of this generation of women we call Silver Birds. The vision of this young and determined woman with a scarf on her head and sleeves rolled up continues to inspire women today with the empowering message "We Can Do It."[1]

"World War II, for many women, was about gaining strength and mobility. As more and more men left to fight in battle, women started taking over traditionally male responsibilities. As far back as history can tell, women have been limited in mobility and set in particular spaces by society, but war changed all the rules. War very much became a doorway through which women ventured out of the homes where they had been confined."[2]

During WWII, women in large numbers were asked to work outside as well as inside the home. For many women, WWII became a symbol of freedom, a time when women no longer were forced into the roles society had created for them. They became free to create their own lives and senses of self. With this increase in freedom also came an increase in equality. WWII gave women the chance to prove they are just as capable as men. And with this new equality and ability to join the workforce, life, as they knew it, changed for women. With money they had earned, they became more independent and confident about their potential. Though relatively short-lived, WWII provided a way for women to do what they wanted. Far fewer obstacles stood in the way of women proving that they were extremely capable. Women are capable of anything; it's too bad that it took a war to make everyone see this.

The Silver Bird women of the 1930s and early 1940s evolved into Silver Bird mothers who were raised to believe that a woman's place was in the home, so they stayed there. These women—who had tasted the bitterness of the Great Depression and the uncertain times of World War II and the sweetness of the postwar boon years—set up house, gave birth, and went about their business in the classic sense of a "traditional" mother. But they did so having had a taste of survival and independence and a heightened awareness of the power of women. So when they returned to the home front, they became the original "residential engineers," running the house and family with proficiency and efficiency and with the knowledge of all that they had achieved during wartime and the suspicion that they could have done even more. As a result, during the 1960s and 1970s, Silver Birds encouraged their daughters to look for satisfaction beyond a white picket fence.

In the 2003 film *Mona Lisa Smile*, actress Julia Roberts plays Professor Katherine Watson, a progressive art professor from California who joins the faculty of conservative Wellesley College in the 1950s; she brings with her new ideas about art and challenges her students' traditional societal roles. Professor Watson exemplifies the Silver Birds suggesting to the Boomers that women could have it all—if only they knew they could ask for it. So boomer women stopped asking permission and started paving a way out of traditional at-home duties and into progressive out-of-home roles. The generation of mothers who had seen firsthand that the shared purpose of a group—rather than the needs and wants of an individual—could accomplish great things reared a generation of mothers who believed that they could make a positive difference in the world. This generation, after all, was the first to experience television and space exploration. Anything was possible. And the daughters who grew to be Baby Boomer mothers responded to the cues of their mothers—whether they were part of the silent majority of at-home mothers or the vocal minority of working women—that they had a choice. A record number of mothers entered the workforce and like a stone skipped on water, created one of the nation's most significant cohort effects.

HATCHING CAREERS

"My mom was always at home. Her job was to be a mom. There was never any question about would she be there when the school bus let you off. Was she happy? I don't think so. But she was good at it," said Kathy Sparrow, 54, a working mother of two teenage sons living in Manteo, North Carolina. When asked whether she struggled about her decision to work rather than follow her mother's path as a stay-at-home mother, Sparrow explained that she never feels a struggle because she believes she's a better parent because she's not an at-home mother. Her career decision allows her to be self-supporting and independent. "I've chosen a direction in my life that allows me to be more independent than what some women have. I'm more fulfilled as a person. I love what I do and I'm good at it. My kids respect me for the fact that I'm good at what I do and that I'm fairly successful in my world," she added.

During the 1960s and 1970s, tens of thousands of boomer women entered the workforce and soon after began having children. A societal clash was bound to happen—and it did. Boomer women became boomer mothers, and, not content to give up their hard-won spoils, they remained in the workforce. As a generation, boomer mothers in the workplace achieved great success. Every generation has a symbol of status. According to demographer Neil Howe, among boomer mothers, "working used to be high status."[3] We hear frequently from boomer mothers that they learned early that rewards could be found in the workplace. They like calling the shots as a boss or managing projects and enjoy being financially compensated for their hard work. Mothers, like nonmom females and Baby Boomer males, matured during a time when conventional values were questioned, women's rights were not yet guaranteed, and the voice of America's youth demanded a seat at the table. The drive for independence and productivity and the chance to be heard had such a profound effect on women that when their time came to enter motherhood, they were reluctant to give up their careers. Ultimately, though, as boomer mothers have the perspective of time, many wonder if the drive to have it all was ever possible.

With the exponential number of mothers in the workforce came an exponential increase in the number of new daycare centers, divorces, and relocations. As job opportunities increased, families became more mobile and geographically spread and no longer able to enjoy the close-knit extended family relationships that came from being geographically desirable.

In her book, *We Are Our Mothers' Daughters,* journalist Cokie Roberts describes mother-daughter tensions that point back to "an inability to consult, or an unwillingness of either mothers or daughters to admit the value of what the other has to say." She goes on to explain, "When mothers who never worked outside the home hear how much their daughters value careers, they take it as a rejection. They are hurt, and often they are jealous as well, feeling they could have 'amounted to something' if they had not devoted themselves to their children. But the daughters don't even seem to give them credit for what they did do—raise a family."[4]

While mother-daughter conflicts may be an age-old problem, Deborah Carr of the University of Michigan Institute for Social Research suggests that Baby Boomer mothers see their daughters as more successful in their professional careers than they are, but few would trade places. "Contrary to what theories would predict, appraising their daughters' professional lives as more successful did not take a toll on the women's self-esteem," she said. "Focusing on the stresses in a daughter's life may allow the mother to justify her own life choices."[5]

Hillary Rodham Clinton's 1996 *New York Times* best-seller, *It Takes A Village,* suggests that in contemporary times, it takes more than a nuclear family structure to properly provide for a child. "Children exist in the world as well as in the family. From the moment they are born, they depend on a host of other 'grown-ups'—grandparents, neighbors, teachers, ministers, employees, political leaders, and untold others who touch their lives directly and indirectly."[6]

Regardless of your political preference or your approval rating for Senator Clinton, what is important is the concept that boomer mothers accepted that "it takes a village" to raise a child. From the early pioneering days, parents looked to their immediate and extended families for support with childcare. As time went by and families moved away from each other, parents were forced to look outward for assistance, marking Boomers as the first generation to develop meaningful nonfamily relationships within their communities.

Baby Boomers led the parade of mothers into the halls of corporate America. As mothers added a new title to their résumés, they added new responsibilities to their roles as mothers. Baby Boomer mothers had to know how to juggle work and family, and in an attempt to do it all, they were forced to reach out to others to help raise their children. Daycare centers grew in number as more and more mothers entered the workplace after giving birth. As these children grew, they were entrusted to care for themselves after school: the "latchkey kid" had arrived. Personal growth was also flourishing. Boomer moms were working hard to penetrate the glass ceiling. They used their unified voice to pass maternity leave policies and ultimately the Family Leave Act in the halls of Congress.

The Vietnam War may have ended, but mothers took up a battle for family-friendly work benefits. Companies appreciated the value working mothers contributed to their bottom lines. The mothers were rewarded with a shrinking disparity between male and female salaries, on-site daycares, and extended maternity leaves. At home, working mothers spent their paychecks on their children, giving them material possessions that exceeded those of their own childhood. They determined that it took a village to raise their children and created support systems to help manage the demands of parenting as they worked long hours at the office. The term *supermom* was born and society recognized a new generation of self-sufficient, multitasking women who could be mothers and CEOs. Progress came with a cost, however.

As the income of women increased, so did the number of divorces. The traditional, nuclear family made way for a new dimension of family, which included stepmothers, half brothers, and single-parent households. The children of this generation suddenly were faced with learning skills that made them more adaptable to the ever-changing aspects of their home life. It also laid the foundation for a generation of skeptical adults. If the most secure environment they knew could be altered, then what else could change unexpectedly in their lives? The answer or lack of it can be seen in the work ethics of those children— Generation Xers of today.

We have begun to see an interesting work style movement emerge among boomer mothers, especially those of young children. The work and family balance approaches of Gen X mothers are being absorbed by boomer mothers, who are tired of trying to have it all right now, and are open to the idea of more fluid work choices. Kathy Sparrow reminds us that over the decades, generational levels have blurred because women have taken so many different paths. A lot of mothers, even those who used to take a traditional path, aren't taking this path, and those who have worked outside the house are looking at ways to be at home more. Some child development experts point to a nation of overindulged children and teenagers as an invitation to parents, mothers especially, to consider flexible work styles. Dan Kindlon, author of *Too Much of a Good Thing: Raising Children of Character in an Indulgent Age,* agrees that parents today are more indulgent than those of the previous generation.[7] Child development experts point to guilt and fatigue as results of working mothers' long hours and the boomer disinclination to deny their children anything.

But how important is it that we understand Baby Boomer moms in the traditional sense of a generation? We believe somewhat. We need to understand the cultural influences that shaped their collective parenting styles and lifestyle choices because that directs us to an understanding of their attitudes and purchasing behaviors. And many of the mothers who are academically members of the cohort share like experiences and thus may tend to raise their children with similar belief systems. However, if you are a marketing director for a packaged-goods company, is it more important that you understand that a Baby Boomer mother wants intellectually charged offspring or that her personal digital assistant (PDA) is the most valuable item in her handbag because she has to keep up with the schedules of three teenagers? The answer is both. Boomer moms may have a newborn or, like Jennifer Murphy, a teen heading off to college.

Boomers are known for their competitive proclivities—moms as much as dads. And they're transferring this zeal for winning, encouraging higher educational standards among their children and performance on the field of play. It is this competitive spirit that has spurred boomer mothers' success at the office. It is this same spirit that encourages them to invest heavily in the intellectual and physical welfare of their children.

Taking into account milestones of the children in a mother's life, we turn our attention to Baby Boomer mothers in the following brackets: mothers of young preschool and school-age children, mothers of teens, and mothers of college students. A series of focus groups held the past year across the country, conducted on behalf of a national consumer electronics retailer, brought into clear focus the distinct needs of a Baby Boomer mother grappling with a variety of life stage events. Mothers of young children, whether working or not, spent considerable energy trying to enrich the lives of their kids by providing every opportunity imaginable as a platform for future success. They purchase interactive learning aids offered by companies such as LeapFrog, sign on for My Gym classes that provide youth-oriented physical fitness activities, and register their progeny for supplemental coursework through programs such as Kumon and Sylvan Learning Centers. They devote their lives to fulfilling the potential of their children, often at the expense of their own needs and pursuits.

As children age, a natural progression begins to take place as those kids become more independent in the world. Lisa Stone of Fit For 2® recognizes this in the way she interprets and defines generations of women. As children age, mothers who temporarily abandoned their own identities experience a natural pull toward latent interests and hobbies or a renewed interest in self-improvement, particularly physical fitness. Astute marketers will find this transition a key time to forge relationships with mothers who are interested in products or services that can bridge their world as mom with their world as an individual. Personal fitness training centers are springing up in retail locations throughout the country to meet the need of aging Baby Boomers, particularly moms, who are willing to pay for one-on-one or small group instruction. Universities and colleges are including an expanded roster of evening courses to respond to mothers' demands for greater intellectual and creative stimulation. Even packaged goods such as teeth-whitening products become important to Baby Boomer mothers as they become more engaged in the world outside of their homes. Recalling our research with the consumer electronics retailer, we found that it was at this time in their lives that Baby Boomer moms showed an increased interest in entertainment content and products. They tend to spend more time and increased dollars on DVD movies and entertainment-focused electronics such as televisions, DVD players, and digital recording devices, including TiVo.

The boomer mom often is more respected when making decisions that relate to home improvement and design based on the wisdom of her years and her experience gathered working on previous homes. It's also at this time that mothers whose children are well on their way to independence venture outside their typical boundaries, either by taking on a new hobby such as photography or hiking, or by reconnecting with friends through girls-only customized travel packages based on interests and location. For more than 20 years, travel agencies like Adventure-Women Travel have been planning such trips for women, and others have followed suit, like http://www.adventurouswench .com, planning experiential trips for women to all corners of the globe. According to the Adventure Women Web site (http:// www.adventurewomen.com), its average customer is 50 years old, married, with one to three children. But with clientele as young as their early 30s, the trend extends beyond Boomers as well.

Ellen Madill, marketing director of Mannington Mills, a leading floor-surfaces manufacturer, believes the impact of the boomer mother to companies who reach out to her is in the longevity of her relationships. "It's important to stay visible to the boomer mother because, as a result of her age and life stage, she is likely to have a wider social network."

A boomer is involved in a broad range of activities related to her many roles as wife, mother, friend, and individual. She might touch other moms in any number of ways during the course of a week at PTA meetings, soccer games, charity events, networking gatherings, super clubs, or gym workouts. As the single largest cohort of mothers today, boomer moms exert vast influence and critical support to a brand's success, and as they impact the world around them, they will also leave their finger-prints on how companies market to mothers at large.

When it comes to marketing to Baby Boomers, it is important to recognize the influences that formulate their values and ultimately drive their behavior as well as their position in this life stage. They are older moms, over the age of 40, who may have pushed childbearing and rearing into their later years, thus representing children of all ages, from newborns to college age. They were the first generation of mothers to take active roles in the workplace and they blazed the trails for the family-friendly work conditions today's Gen X and Gen Y mothers experience. After many years of martyrdom, they are now enjoying the rewards of their labors and high purchasing power. Their disposable income makes them a very important segment of the Mom Market. Perhaps the most important revelation in this chapter is that boomer moms are more likely to adapt their behavior as parents to the behavior of mothers who share the same-age children. To increase the effectiveness of their marketing strategies, companies should focus on the age of the child rather than on the age of the mother. As Baby Boomer moms continue to age, their value as consumers will grow incrementally as they influence the buying decisions not only for their families, companies, and peers, but also for their aging parents. Connecting with this cohort with the right message will mean increased sales and market share for brands that win the hearts of these moms.

5

GEN X MARKS THE SPOT

Generation X has had so much negative media attention that we almost feel bad talking about them yet again. Fortunately, the wealth of knowledge this generation can provide to marketers is so valuable that we will add our names of those who attempt to describe a generation labeled only with an X. The name Generation X was coined by a young Canadian author, Douglas Coupland, who in a 1990 nonfiction novel, *Generation X: Tales for An Accelerated Culture,* termed his generation *Gen Xers.* At the time of his book, he was dissatisfied with all the labels Baby Boomers had used to identify his generation.

Generation X moms, born between 1965 and 1976, currently are 28 to 39 years old. They number approximately 51 million and as a whole represent approximately 25 percent of the population.[1] Generation X is particularly difficult to generalize because it is the most diverse generation in history. It is made up of more ethnic backgrounds than any of its predecessors. Generation X is the largest population of naturalized citizens in U.S. history.[2]

Thanks to negative and often unfounded media coverage that depicted Gen Xers as lazy, whiny, cynical, and disloyal, one common theme exists within this group of men and women. They hate to be called Xers. Quite possibly the most misunderstood generation, this group has long been important to marketers, but it remains difficult to define and reach. We strive to change that in the next few pages and give you the tool to capture this generation's lucrative spending.

Until September 11, Generation X was the only generation not to have witnessed a powerful life-changing event such as a war or a major natural disaster. Unlike Baby Boomers who were polarized by the Vietnam War and the death of John F. Kennedy, this cohort did not have a binding issue. The only war they experienced was the Persian Gulf War, which they watched live on CNN, witnessing firsthand bombs exploding behind Bernard Shaw as he reported from a balcony in Kuwait City, halfway around the globe.

As we discussed in prior chapters, the influence and roles of their mothers may have played the largest part in shaping this generation.

THE LATCHKEY KIDS

Generation Xers are also known as the generation of "latch-key kids," a description for children of working mothers who symbolically carried keys around their necks so they could let themselves into their homes after school. These children had to become self-reliant and fend for themselves while their boomer mothers worked long hours away from home. The outcome of these long hours spent alone produced a generation that grew up confident in their problem-solving abilities. This skill will become apparent when we later examine the parenting style of Generation X mothers. Their time at home was spent watching MTV or playing the first video games to enter the market, including Pong and Pacman. They became comfortable making decisions on their own and finding solutions to problems while their parents were at work. Most important, they watched their mothers work hard to find a balance between their family duties and their careers.

GENERATION OF DIVORCE

One of the greatest influences of this generation was divorce. This was the first generation since the Beaver Cleaver household of the 1950s to have to learn to manage divorced parents, splitting their time between two households and developing relationships with blended families. Some experts estimated that nearly half of Gen Xers grew up in divorced households, based on the census number that 50 percent of marriages in the late 1960s and 1970s ended in divorce. To fully appreciate the family environment this generation experienced, one just has to look at the numbers. The divorce rate tripled since 1960; the number of children born out of wedlock increased by 28 percent during the same time period; and the number of absent fathers also went up.[3] After years of being left home alone, Gen Xers found that the security of their family life was rocked by divorce. The result was a universal longing to create a secure environment for themselves within the uncertain framework of life.

One effect of the uncertainty they witnessed among their parents was their lack of desire to get married. According the 2000 census, single mothers make up the fastest-growing demographic in the United States.[4] Surprisingly, this group is not the result of increased divorce but rather of new moms' decisions to postpone marriage, regardless of unplanned pregnancies. In addition, the freedom to stay single is made easier by the Generation X mom's ability to financially support her family's needs on her own.

To witness firsthand this generation's attitudes on marriage and commitment, one only has to turn on the hottest sitcoms. Thursday night prime time is filled with story lines in which twentysomething friends sit around in groups in coffee shops, hesitant to commit to another person. Or tune in to a show focused on the plight of divorcees challenged to blend two families. It's a long way from *Leave It to Beaver* that entertained Baby Boomers or *The Brady Bunch* and *Happy Days* episodes that entertained Gen Xers after school while they were growing up. Generation Xers are cautious romantics who defer marriage in hopes of creating a stable family environment in the future. Without a young family to nurture, these women are turning to education to further their career possibilities and, in the process, are becoming increasingly financially independent. It's a cycle that eliminates the need to marry to become a mother.

WELCOME HOME XERS

There's an old adage that a mother's job is never done and thanks to Generation Xers, this has never been truer. Because they are deferring marriage, many Gen Xers are returning home after college to their boomer moms who once considered themselves empty nesters. In her book, *The Postponed Generation: Why America's Grown-up Kids Are Growing Up Later,* Susan Littwin illustrates how differently Baby Boomers reacted to graduation. In 1970, only 47 percent of Boomers between 18 and 24 lived with their parents; in 1992, a record 54 percent of Xers between 18 and 24 lived with theirs. In 1975, the median age for first marriages among Boomers was 23.5 for men and 21.1 for women; in 1992, the median age for first Gen Xer marriages was 26.5 for men and 24.4 for women.[5]

This new living pattern means they are extending the influence of their parents and repositioning their roles within that relationship. Suddenly, mom and dad are taking on the role of friend and mentor with their young adult offspring. We will see that later this new relationship with their mothers will affect Gen Xers when they become mothers themselves. When it comes to marketing to Gen X moms, therefore, their mothers exert a greater influence in their parenting styles and buying decisions. They no longer see mom in the negative role of "Mom knows best" but as a mom who can provide valuable input in the decision-making process. Although most moms will solicit the advice of their own mothers after giving birth for the first time, the relationship moves from simply mother-daughter to a friendship based on the common experience of motherhood, and the mother's advice carries double the weight. Because of the nature of Gen Xers to be self-reliant and create their own solutions, however, they would ultimately make their own decisions based on what's right for them personally. They will still give their mothers' opinions priority over those of friends or other family members. In a recent survey conducted for a client on choosing a method of feeding babies, almost 80 percent of new mothers said they turned to their mothers for comforting words of advice while pregnant.

Let's look at how this plays out in the decision-making process of a Gen X mom deciding on the type of baby food to feed her new baby. She will turn to her friends or members of a peer group and ask them to share their personal stories and experiences with various brands. Gen X moms like stories because they illustrate the individuality of different situations. They allow her to see that there is more than one way to do things. Once she gets insights from peers, she'll test this information with her mother. Not surprisingly, the Baby Boomer grandmother will tell her how things were when she was a child and what brands she used to feed her babies as a young mother. The Gen X mom will discount stories of the "old days" in an attempt to forget her own unstable childhood and avoid re-creating it for her child. What changes the scenario is that the Gen X mom, who has now repositioned her mother as a friend rather than just her mom, will extrapolate the valuable facts from her mother's advice. Now the influence of "Well, I turned out OK so it must work" that she denotes from the conversation with her mother is weighed against the advice she perceives from the same conversation with her mom as a friend. This makes her mom's opinion twice as influential to the Gen X mom as it was to any other generation of mothers. This does not mean that brands that fared well with boomer moms will automatically become best sellers. Although these brands have the advantage of receiving grandma's approval, they must reinvent themselves and their messages to capture the attention of the younger Gen X moms. As we will soon discover, it takes more than a strong brand to gain the loyalty of this media-savvy and skeptical generation.

THE QUEST FOR INDIVIDUALITY

Generation Xers are on a quest for individuality. They feel that being their own person allows them to better control the uncertainties of the world they experienced as a child. Many of us can remember the days of punk rockers, extensive tattoos, and ears that were adorned with more than one earring. All were statements of independence expressed by Generation X.

The quest for individuality is seen on retail shelves with the popularity of personalized jewelry, sweaters, stationery, and household items. Last year's fashion trends featured purses with large initials monogrammed on them, oversize jeweled letters, and shirts bearing large initials similar to Laverne's legendary L in the *Laverne & Shirley* television sitcom. This presents an interesting challenge for big-box retailers such as Wal-Mart and Target to find a way to market products to a consumer base that desires personal, more customized merchandise. We will offer suggestions for mastering this clash between mass marketing and Generation X mom's style.

We believe that the appeal of home improvement will continue to grow with Generation X mothers. Not only does a new coat of paint enable a mom to express her individuality, but it also allows her to utilize the problem-solving abilities she mastered in childhood. Another area that permits the Generation X mother to express her creativity is cooking, thus the popularity of cooking shows with young adults. A stick of butter, a cup of flour, and an egg can be a myriad of items when mixed with a bit of that and a pinch of this. And the idea of a family sitting down to a delicious home-cooked meal speaks to the Gen X mother's desire to create the stable family life she yearns for. It is this quest for stability that we will discuss next.

CREATING STABILITY

A stable home life is the dream of many Generation Xers—particularly those who grew up either as latchkey children or as the products of divorce. Supposedly, everything will eventually come back into style, and this also may be true for the traditional nuclear family. A vision of the Cleaver family may come to mind, but once again we ask you to place your preconceived ideas of mom aside. The stable home life for a Generation Xer may or may not include all the personalities of the Cleaver family. Don't tell Ward, but his mandatory role as the head of the household was lost during Y2K. Today's Generation X mom wants to create stability for herself and her children with or without a man. The effects of her upbringing make her flexible and adaptable. If she finds a man she trusts to complement her family, she will marry. But if not, she is willing and able to raise her children on her own. Ultimately, she holds herself responsible for creating a secure environment for herself and her children, both currently and in the future. While Baby Boomer moms believed it took a village to raise a child, Generation X moms believe it takes a family.

It's also important to note that the Generation X moms' quest for stability extends beyond their homes. They expect life to be balanced with leisure time, comfortable clothing in the workplace, enriching experiences, and the option to work from home. The instability of the latter has led these moms to redefine work.

THE NEW DEFINITION OF WORK

Downsizing, restructuring, and *outsourcing* were the new terms used in their parents' workplaces. Generation Xers watched their working mothers and fathers lose their jobs, after years of tenure with their employers. The same parents who demonstrated loyalty to their employers and looked forward to departing only after receiving a gold watch and retirement luncheon were thrown by the wayside as corporations traded employee loyalty for improved bottom lines. Gen Xers also witnessed scandals such as Watergate, the shrinking of Social Security benefits in the future, and decreasing health benefits. All this contributed to distrust in institutions and long-standing relationships with employers.

These influences, along with their learned ability to be self-reliant, created an entrepreneurial spirit among Generation Xers. Their childhood experience of finding solutions and creating opportunities gives them confidence in exploring new challenges and a greater sense of independence. The term *slacker* couldn't be less appropriate for this group of young people who started more businesses at a young age than previous generations did.

Generation Xers look at the workplace as a destination of learning. They see companies not as places to retire, but as resources for networking and for learning new skills, which can help them move up the pay scale and the employment ladder. Their loyalty to their employer is limited by the benefits they perceive they will receive in return. Because Gen Xers are valuable employees with much to contribute, employers must attract and retain them by presenting visible career paths, elevated training programs, and intellectually engaging work environments. In the workplace, they require instant gratification and an outlet to express their individuality.

When Generation Xers become mothers, they recognize the need to work to provide for their families. Their desire to create a stable environment for their children increases their sense of accountability to the family and the household spending. They desire jobs that allow them to provide for their children and to nurture them as well. In fact, they expect it. This generation watched their own mothers blaze the trails in establishing flextime and telecommuting. They know these are options and feel entitled to them. The downside for companies who wish to retain these valuable employees is that in addition to their technology skills, they possess a refined talent for creating their own solutions. They don't need to wait for an employer to create an

Generation X Likes and Dislikes in the Workplace[6]

Likes	Dislikes
Honesty	Hearing about the past
Feedback (praise or suggestion to improve)	Inflexibility
Visuals	Over-managed approach/ Limiting thinking
Speak in plain, straightforward terms	Disparaging comments about their generation
Continuous development	Disrespect by not making the point clear
Balance between work and personal time	Judged by the number of hours they work
Focus on results	Focus on technique
Involvement in decisions	Bureaucratic layers
Fun—celebrate the successes	No recognition or rewards

attractive option that meets their needs; they may just as easily take themselves out of their workplaces and into home-based offices or companies of their own.

In the simplest terms, if a Generation X mother doesn't find satisfaction working for you, she will find what she needs elsewhere or on her own.

RELIGION AND SPIRITUALITY

In an unlikely shift, Generation Xers are turning to religion. The skepticism that produces distrust in long-established institutions is being overshadowed by other factors. Kevin Ford in *Jesus for a New Generation*[7] points to several characteristics in Gen Xers that make them open to spirituality. First is their interest in the supernatural. "Xers tend to believe in transcendent realities, but they also like to pour their energies and their bodies into a spiritual experience of the here and now. They differ from their more scientifically grounded predecessors in this manner. Second is their interest in death." Ford illustrates this characteristic with Gen Xers' fascination with experiencing death-based games such as Dungeons & Dragons and Area 51 and books such as *Final Exit*. He also points to the interest they have in dark comedies and research on Satan. Some of this interest may be the result of the access they have to technology and information on the Internet. The growth of virtual communities makes it easy for seekers with similar interests to compare beliefs and trade inner thoughts without the inhibitions of face-to-face communications. The final characteristic Ford points to is the Gen Xers' search for reality. He confirms the observation that this generation wants to control their world and find solutions for handling difficult family challenges. "They need a faith that works in the conflicts, pressures, and pain of their everyday lives," says Ford.[8]

A survey conducted by *Group Magazine* found that most Xers dislike the established religious institutions but do believe in God. The distaste for the structures of faith, but not the faith itself, stems from their distaste of hypocrites, limited thinking, and conformity. Finding spiritual fulfillment is more important to Generation Xers than being involved in a church or other house of worship.[9] Fueling the skepticism about the church are the numerous religious leader scandals witnessed firsthand by this generation. The fall of Jim and Tammy Faye Bakker and Jerry Falwell as well as scandals in the Catholic Church are just a few that have left a taste of distrust in the minds of this generation. In addition, popular games such as Dungeon & Dragons and characters like Van Helsing have spawned an interest in the darker side of spirituality.

Successful religious marketers have identified Gen Xers' reliance on technology. They are creating technology-savvy churches that offer e-mail sermons, virtual communities of prayer groups, and online scripture readings. The names of these churches—Warehouse 242 and Spirit Garage among others—reflect the hip audience to whom they cater. PlayStation and Xbox games bring alive the Goth characters of *The Crow* and *The Blair Witch Project*, building a stronger relationship with the unreal.

GATHERING GENERATION XERS

Generation Xers hold high expectations for groups. They like to form and belong to groups where they can share ideas and find opportunities for growth, creating surrogate families of like-minded peers who share their vision of community and chosen family. With unlimited groups that exist for just about every interest, personal value, or belief, whether in person or virtually, Gen Xers can express their individuality and find common ground with others across the city or across the country. Because technology continues to fuel Gen Xers' ability to express themselves in different ways and establish connections in ways that are comfortable for them, it is of paramount importance in their daily lives. and they are therefore very comfortable with existing and new technologies. This is important to recognize as we explore the opportunities to market to Gen X mothers online through chat rooms and virtual communities. The types of groups in which they participate, such as book clubs, running teams, or support groups, matter less than what they do with them. The socializing allows them to express their personal views, learn from their peers, and gain acceptance on their terms. The popularity of groups among this generation can be witnessed in the popular sitcom, *Friends,* whose core characters are single Gen Xers who gather regularly to exchange ideas, share real-life stories, and act as a family unit. Groupings by Xers have spawned myriad new social interactions among all generations. They include Mommy and Me playgroups, Bible study groups, volunteering events, and home parties. In fact, the home party plan business has grown to a $29.95 billion industry.[10]

While Baby Boomers bought Avon one-on-one with a beauty consultant, Gen X moms today purchase everything from lingerie to cookware to candles in the company of other moms in a friendly living room setting.

MOTHER X

The influence of education is perhaps one of the most notable parenting priorities among Generation X mothers. As you might recall, these moms consider education an important tool for creating opportunities for stability for themselves and their children. Generation X moms value education, which can be seen in several aspects of their parenting. First, this is apparent with the toys she purchases for her child. The most popular items today carry some type of educational benefit. Companies such as LeapFrog, Touch Books, and Baby Einstein have made millions on Gen Xers' desire to give their children a head start on learning. During a recent research project for a consumer product client, we asked new mothers if they witnessed other moms pushing their babies to learn at earlier-than-expected ages. More than 85 percent said they have witnessed such behavior in their peers. Ironically, only 33 percent admitted doing it themselves, which means it's not something they are proud of doing. Generation X moms prefer to spend money on enriching experiences that will create family memories such as unique vacations and adventure travel.

It's not enough to buy airline tickets and spend nights in a posh resort. Now the experience must include something to enhance the vacation for every member of the family. Delta's low-fare provider, Song, has followed this lead by creating a new flying experience for moms. "While Song has introduced fresh, organic salads, sandwiches and wraps, Bonterra organic wines, personal bottles of Dasani water, and flight attendant uniforms designed by kate spade to help mom enjoy *her* experience, the amenities she appreciates *most* from Song tend to be that her husband can enjoy an Amstel Light while watching live sports on ESPN as her tween drinks a Coke and listens to MP3s and her eight-year-old munches on a snack from Dylan's Candy Bar while watching the Cartoon Network. Counter to the adage, 'Ain't momma happy, ain't nobody happy,' mom only *really* relaxes when she knows everyone else in the family is well cared for. If you want to make *mom* happy, make her *family* happy," says Tim Mapes, Managing Director of Marketing for Song Airways.

Gen Xers are active consumers. They weigh their buying decisions against the personal and financial costs they set for themselves. In other words, before purchasing a product or service, they will decide if it's worth it for them in the investment of time and/or dollars. They are very realistic and define value against their sense of realism. They can't be sold and see marketing at face value, looking past flash and sizzle to make purchases based on their own needs. They want results and benefits, plain and simple. Their pragmatic attitude on life appears in what they expect from marketers. They want real answers to real-life challenges. And this grounding in reality and the desire to speak the truth has birthed the new genre of television entertainment—reality television—and the increased interest in live broadcasts, eliminating the ability of someone behind the scenes to manipulate the story or the outcome. Remember, this group watched the Persian Gulf War begin and end on CNN.

Marketers need to adapt their institutions—that is, retail locations and service methods—to create engaging experiences for Gen Xers. Marketers need to find ways to involve Gen Xers in the activity of buying. Best Buy has done a good job of this by creating its mom-friendly stores as part of a project called "Jill Stores." In these retail locations, moms can let their children try out the latest technology-based toys in comfortable play stations that sport low seating for the children. Additionally, Best Buy has created store destinations that reflect a mom's real world: the kitchen with letter magnets on the door of the refrigerator, a living room with an oversize couch and big-screen TV, and a children's playroom outfitted with the latest Best Buy merchandise. This approach presents Gen X moms with choices that allow her to take control of her buying decisions in a realistic environment that builds her trust in the company by demonstrating that it understands her, her family, and her lifestyle.

Gen Xers are visual in their learning, a trait learned while watching TV and exploring the early years of computer games and activities. They enjoy imagery but recognize that it is just an outcome of technology. They may appreciate the gloss of a high-dollar Super Bowl ad, but they recognize that a brand is not its image but how it performs. This way of thinking allows them to be cautious with their money.

Their ability to juggle tasks, a skill they learned as latchkey kids, enables them to absorb multimedia messages at one time.

They have the mental capacity to take in and process images that are being delivered to them through multiple channels. Marketers are responding to this by creating online marketing initiatives that include instant messages combined with music downloads.

Although their childhoods created a sense of uncertainty, Gen X moms tend to be traditionalists perhaps as a way to create stability for their children. The resurrection of nostalgic toys, games, and retro designs has in large part been fueled by the Gen Xer's desire to hold on to a conservative traditional family life. For this reason, games such as Parcheesi, Twister, Hi Ho! Cherry-O, and Connect Four have topped the list of hot sellers for the past several holiday seasons.

One company that has leveraged its brand and product offering well with Generation X moms is *Highlights for Children* magazine. In 1999, the 75-year-old magazine company launched Highlights-Jigsaw, a home party plan company that offers quality educational toys. All products are sold through Product Advisors who are home-based business owners that sell Highlights-Jigsaw toys, games, and books at home parties called Talkabouts. These are high-quality toys associated with a nostalgic brand. What child doesn't remember receiving *Highlights* magazine with its famous Timbertoes family and hidden picture puzzles? The company offers Generation X moms many solutions that meet their core values. Highlights-Jigsaw products provide educational tools for their children by providing a flexible, part-time business opportunity; creating a shopping experience with a group of moms in a social environment; and offering the chance to educate themselves in a way that will enhance the life and learning of their children. The company is perfectly positioned to leverage the Generation X Mom Market.

"Home-based businesses allow moms to be with their children and still contribute income to the household. Many women search not only for a home business, but for one that is a genuine 'fit' with their family," explains Pat Mikelson, President of

Highlights-Jigsaw. "One of the great side benefits of being involved with educational toys is the joy our Advisors get from using the toys, games, and puzzles with their own children. These moms clearly value the opportunity to learn how to enrich their children's learning development. They feel great as they play with their children and experience the many 'Look! I did it!' exclamations that we all love to hear from our children."

Mikelson says it's important for the business to provide a worthwhile service or product that truly benefits society. She recalls a day that a dad expressed it this way, "I work in corporate America and that is my 'job', but my wife's Highlights-Jigsaw business really has a soul."

The value Generation X moms put on education is apparent in their focus on saving for their children's future educational needs. A study by Alliance Capital Management revealed that 68 percent of Gen Xer parents were setting money aside for their children's college education, compared to 51 percent of Boomers between 25 and 49.[11] The average Gen X moms and dads start putting money away for college when their baby is two and a half, while most Boomers wait until their' baby is seven.[12] We have long preached about the opportunities that exist for financial institutions within the Mom Market, and with the growing number of fiscally responsible Gen X moms, these opportunities increase as well. More opportunities exist for banks, investment firms, and financial planners to step forward and engage Gen X moms with products and programs that meet their needs. Generation Xers also recognize that financial security can be obtained by developing good saving habits early and establishing relationships with knowledgeable professionals.

Banks and other financial institutions can capitalize on this emerging market of women by creating new products designed with their needs in mind. For instance, ask any mother how often she forgets to pay her child's allowance and most will snicker. Either she doesn't have change for a $20 or completely forgets until reminded by her son or daughter. A creative solution for this mom is a bank that offers a child's allowance account that automatically moves money from her account to the child's account weekly. This would not only help to retain the mom as a customer but would establish a banking relationship with the child at an early age. There is also an opportunity for a financial services company to establish itself as a leader in helping moms teach their children financial responsibility. This is an area of learning that moms receive little coaching in but one in which help would be greatly appreciated.

Finally, it is important to mention the significance of music in the life of a Generation Xer, particularly in a marketing book. Gen Xers like stories. Stories about themselves give them their identity. Music plays a major role in telling these stories. Gen Xers are so diverse in their taste in music because it fluctuates with the types of stories they want to tell. Singers such as Eminem express their rebellion from (against) established institutions, while Norah Jones helps them sing their blues. The ability to download select songs from a particular artist, instead of having to buy an entire CD, provides Gen Xers with further flexibility in creating the soundtracks of their lives.[13]

In this chapter, we gained a better understanding of a generation that has touted the distinction of being largely misunderstood. For those marketers who convince Gen Xers they appreciate skeptical views on life and the quest to create a secure home life for children, there is a valuable segment of mom consumers to be won. Gen X moms want companies to recognize their desire for solutions, whether products or services, that facilitate their integrated lifestyle. They want to simplify home and work to spend more time with their children and they expect companies to partner with them to reach these goals. Successful marketing initiatives will capitalize on this generation's high comfort level with technology and the need for information during the buying decision process. Gen Xer marketing messages will reflect this generation's desire for personalization. Brands will allow these moms to express their individuality by offering creative solutions, innovative product selection, and multiple delivery channels. Although they rank fewer in numbers to Baby Boomers and Gen Ys, Generation X mothers are an important segment of mothers to capture because many are now in their prime childbearing years. Marketers who connect on the right level with Gen X moms will enjoy a loyal relationship that will add up to big bucks.

6

GENERATION Y NOT?

If Generation X was short on descriptive names, Generation Y has more than its share. Members of Generation Y are known as the Echo Boomers, the Digital Generation, Generation Next, and, more commonly, the Millennials. Born between 1977 and 1994, they are most often defined by the fact that they graduated from high school in the new millennium. In 2004, they are 10 to 27 years old. They number 70 million and make up 21 percent of the U.S. population.[1] For marketers, Generation Y presents the largest consumer group to emerge since the Baby Boomer generation. It is estimated that the population will grow by twice the rate as Generation Y continues to increase until 2010. As a consumer group, this generation controls approximately $172 billion a year and influences $300 billion in family spending annually.[2]

Gen Y has enjoyed a prosperous childhood. American Girl Dolls, with a price tag of almost $100 each, adorn the beds of tween girls, while teenagers hang out in bedrooms stylishly decorated from Pottery Barn catalogs. More than two-thirds of these teenagers have televisions in their rooms, and when they aren't absorbing media visually, 70 percent of them are online. Times are good for today's teenagers. Generation Ys of 2004, whether affluent or not, own a cell phone, PlayStation, and DVD player, and they travel to places like Cancún, Jamaica, and Puerto Rico for spring break. The average teenager receives an allowance of more than $80 a week and two-thirds have savings accounts.[3] We were amused to learn the number one adjective used to describe Generation Y mothers is—"spoiled." This term was given to this generation not only by Gen X and boomer moms, but it was noted by Generation Ys themselves. Moms describe Gen Y moms as we have described them as a generation, as the benefactors of the prosperity of Baby Boomer moms. They've enjoyed interacting with brands otherwise seen as luxury items to

G*eneration Y Snapshot*[5]

Smoking, drinking, and drug use fell simultaneously in 2002 for the first time ever. (University of Michigan's Institute of Social Research)

The national suicide rate among teenagers has fallen. (National Center for Health Statistics, United States)

Volunteerism is on the rise. A University of California (UCLA) survey of college freshmen from the fall of 2001 showed an all-time high of 86.2 percent who reportedly engaged in volunteer work, compared to 66 percent in 1989.

Participation in church groups among teens rose from 17 percent to 28 percent between 1995 and 2001. (Roper) (brandchannel.com)

Violent crime by 12- to 17-year-olds is down by 50 percent from its 1993 peak. (U.S. Bureau of Justice Statistics)

Overall teen sexual activity has declined and virginity is on a rise. (Centers for Disease Control and Prevention)

others: Coach, Miu Miu, Dooney & Burke, John Hardy, and David Yurman. Boomer moms, those mothers of today's Gen Y women, substituted the time they spent with their children by making them the object of the money they earned while away at work. In other words, moms who felt like they needed to justify their pursuit of a career often did so saying they wanted to give their children the things they wanted for themselves. Now you have a generation of young women who get manicures at age 12 and enjoy $3 lattes before going off to high school.

They are the most socioeconomic and ethnically diverse population in the history of the United States. Minorities make up 34 percent of Generation Y, up from 24 percent in the Baby Boomer cohort.[4] It is interesting to note that by 2010, Hispanics will be the largest minority group in this generation. Gen Y is a well-blended generation that celebrates diversity and, in general, supports change that furthers inclusiveness and equality, such as accepting gay marriage.

GROWING UP WITH THE GOOD LIFE

Unlike the prior generation, Generation Y experienced several influential events that defined and united its members. These include the Columbine shootings, the O. J. Simpson live car chase and subsequent trial, the death of Princess Diana, and, of course, the Monica Lewinsky and President Clinton scandal and presidential impeachment proceedings. Topping the list of these major events, however, is September 11. The events of that day branded the hearts of all Americans, but only this generation experienced the vulnerability of the United States as children. Philosophers often profess that out of bad, good can be born, and Generation Y may be on its way to proving this true. Instead of creating a generation of bitter and angry individuals, the tragic events of 2001 created a spirit of optimism, a passion for creating a better place to live, and an understanding of the state of the world beyond their front yards. We will examine the implications of this later in this chapter, along with the impact of their mothers' influence on the choices this generation will make as future mothers.

Children of moms who played on the floor with them, Generation Ys are the children of late Baby Boomers and early Generation X mothers. Although three out of four Gen Ys have a working mother, their mothers are quite different from those who raised the latchkey children of the prior generation.[6] These mothers turned their attention to nurturing their young rather than chasing material possessions and career titles. These are the mothers who enjoyed movies like *Three Men and a Baby* and *Baby Boom*, which depicted nurturing parents who made rearing children the focus of their lives and then ended up enriched by the experience. They have a sincere interest in parenting in a style we describe as "get on the floor and play." As their children got older, they shuttled them from activity to activity, hoping to give them enrichment in areas of the arts, academics, and athletics. While mothers of Baby Boomers lived by the whip, mothers of Generation Y believed in sparing the rod, becoming the first generation of mothers not to believe in spanking. Dr. Benjamin Spock no longer was their guide, and instead they turned to experts such as T. Berry Brazelton, Elizabeth Pantley, and Dr. William Sears. Rather than merely issuing a punishment to their children, these mothers asked for their children's involvement in the process. Mothers of Generation Y can often be heard saying to their children, "I understand you were angry when you hit your babysitter" or "It is frustrating to be missing a puzzle piece," in an attempt to validate their children's feelings before correcting the situations. Generation Y children were taught to understand the way they felt about elements within their environment and to respond with an appropriate amount of individualism. This new style of parenting was designed to boost a child's self-confidence by validating his or her feelings at an early age.

Dr. Roni Leiderman, Associate Dean for Mailman Segal Institute for Early Childhood Studies at Nova Southeastern University, explains the new style of parenting that younger moms are utilizing to raise their children: "There is a move from the more traditional approach that includes spanking and punishment to the more liberal approaches that are permissive and nonpunitive. While our society has recognized that physically reprimanding a child is inappropriate yet simultaneously understanding that giving a child the run of the house was not effective, parents were not given alternatives to effectively handle their discipline challenges. The style of parenting that is respectful and reflective, that recognizes a child's feelings while giving clear boundaries and consequences for misbehavior, offers a viable approach that works. Although this orientation takes practice, requires more self-reflection, and needs more patience to see results, parents feel like they have a tool that is both effective and respectful to their children."

You might say that Generation Y was a very coddled group of babies. Almost every approach to parenting this group was based on building self-esteem. Generation Y was raised by mothers who believe building self-confidence in their children was the greatest gift they could give their children. These babies were the first graduates of Mommy and Me classes, which promoted play and praise. From a very young age, these children were told they could be or do anything they imagined and they grew up to believe it. This theme has remained with them as they matured. Along the way, Gen Ys were applauded when they took their first steps and cheered on the multiple athletic fields they played on after school. They were encouraged to try new things and build on talents they discovered along the way. Mothers of Generation Ys can be proud that they succeeded in raising confident young adults. Self-confidence is one of the most defining traits of this generation, producing a spirit of ambition and passion that is illustrated in numerous areas. We will examine many in this chapter. Other less flattering characteristics were also spawned by this era of confidence. Gen Ys are perceived by some researchers as possessing an air of superiority that belittles other generations. This attitude can be seen in the television shows that are most popular with these young people. Shows such as *Fairly Odd Parents, Jimmy Neutron, That's So Raven,* and *Super Babies: Baby Geniuses 2* all feature peers with supersized intelligence or extraordinary skills that allow them to outsmart adults.

Gen Ys are also aware of the damage caused by previous generations to their world, and have grown up in a more environmentally sensitive climate than any previous generation. Educated about the differences between organic and conventional foods and natural choices from shampoos to cold remedies, these children consider the previous alternative ways of living as mainstream. The popularity of electronic vehicles (EVs) is just a sign that these young environmentalists are concerned with making the world a better place to live.

Self-assured Gen Ys believe they can change the world and correct the problems caused by the less capable generations that came before them. When it comes to government and social issues, they seem to mimic Generation Xers in their laid-back nature and technology-driven solutions, but they mirror the idealism of the Baby Boomers. They are optimistic, committed, ambitious, and passionate about issues, whether regarding the environment or putting more EVs on the road.

TEENS TODAY, HEROES TOMORROW

Neil Howe and William Strauss, authors of *Millennials Rising: The Next Great Generation,* say Generation Ys will be a "hero" generation like their World War II grandparents. The authors predict "they will be a generation capable of rebuilding powerful political and economic institutions and reenergizing a sense of community and public purpose."[7] Teenagers today are more interested and active in politics than the preceding generation, and they likely will continue to be active in government. While Gen Xers distrusted institutions and leadership, Gen Ys tend to trust authority figures. In an often-sited statistic revealed in a Roper survey, today's teens claim that their parents are their heroes and that they enjoy spending time with them. This close relationship with their own parents greatly influences the relationships they have with other authority figures.

We believe that another factor in Gen Ys interest in government and social services is the foundation of volunteerism that has been a part of their young lives. As mentioned before, many high schools require students to perform a mandatory number of volunteer hours for graduation eligibility, while colleges now measure community volunteerism as entrance criteria. Additionally, the Internet has brought global issues to the screens of millions of tweens and teens. The perception that the impact of hunger, AIDS, and poverty is so close motivates young people to react. Coupled with their confidence to evoke change, Generation Ys are well positioned to shape the future of our country as technology brings social issues to their doorsteps.

TECHNOCULTURE

Technology has played a major role in shaping all aspects of the life of Generation Ys. In fact, this was the first generation born into technology. From the time of their birth, they played with high-tech toys such as LeapFrog and watched Baby Einstein educational videos. By the time they were toddlers, many were on computers with Reader Rabbit, Disney.com, and Fisher-Price. As they grew, their use of technology grew with them. Seventy-three percent of 12- to 17-year-olds have Internet access at home or at school.[8] In fact, 60 percent of all households with children under age 7 have a computer in the home and 67 percent use it regularly.[9] Recent research by the Fortino Group estimates that the current population of 10- to 17-year-olds will spend one-third of their lives on the Internet. Two-thirds of all children under 18 have televisions in their bedrooms.[10] They are using technology to learn, communicate, and make purchases. Jupiter Communications reports that 67 percent of 13- to 18-year-olds and 37 percent of 5- to 12-year-olds have researched or bought products online, and that annual e-commerce sales to Gen Y customers totaled $1.3 billion in 2002.[11]

Perhaps one of the most formative uses of technology is in socializing with friends. Communicating with peers has long been a popular activity with teens, but while Boomers spent hours telephoning girlfriends and Gen Xers later used e-mail, Instant Messaging is today's technology of choice. In fact, two-thirds of teenagers use Instant Messaging,[12] Next time you are traveling on business during the summer, take a peek at the hotel business center at night to see just who is online. You will likely find vacationing teens Instant Messaging friends back home so that they don't miss a thing while they are away. The use of technology has created a generation that is always connected to friends, family, and information. For this reason, Gen Ys move and operate in groups whether physically or virtually. The constant accesses these young people have to the relationships they value have instilled a sense of strong loyalty among their cohorts. The importance they place on loyalty to their friends is seen in the popular movies of 2004. *Lilo & Stitch* and *Finding Nemo* both portrayed the theme that "no one is left behind." The main characters remain with their friends, regardless of pending perils, out of loyalty.

WORKING ON NEW TERMS

The loyalty, ambition, and passion that Generation Ys possess make them valuable workplace assets. Their attitudes toward work relate more closely to their Gen X predecessors than to those of the Baby Boomers. Gen Ys are not driven by the

promise of financial reward. Instead they focus on life as a multifaceted experience, with work being just a piece of what defines them. Flextime, part-time hours, and telecommuting are
givens to this group as they feel entitled to create a work experience that fits their lifestyles and needs. This group has never
known a workforce completely dominated by men, because they
are too young to remember the Baby Boomers' struggles to be
accepted in the corporate world and their attempts to hide their
femininity in order to break through the glass ceiling. The
choice of a job is based more on Gen Ys' lifestyles rather than
on long-term career plans. They look at their personal needs
and then select work accordingly. Keep in mind that members
of this generation were told they could be anything and they
are confident with that thought. With the knowledge that they
can achieve anything they set their minds to, they decide what
they want to be and use their ambition and confidence to find
the perfect professional opportunity. We will see later that this
decision-making process applies to purchases as well.

They value hard work. Nearly half of Generation Y teenagers have part-time jobs.[13] Their work ethic is established at a
very early age, based on the time and effort they put into activities and schoolwork. Compare the daily schedules of some
teens against their working parents' hour for hour, and you'll
find that many actually put in longer days than their parents
do. A typical middle-school student will arrive at school between
6:30 and 8 AM, while mom gets to the office by 8:30 AM. The
schoolday might end at 3:30 or 4 PM and then it's time for extracurricular activities. Athletic practices, volunteer hours, and
homework must be crammed into the afternoon, leaving minimal time for dinner and leisure time before going to bed. The
good news is that Generation Ys value hard work because their
success has always been met with praise from their mothers.
They know that hard work will pay off, in one way or another.

At work, their social tendencies help them thrive in group
settings. They will show loyalty to the other members of their

team and their solution-oriented mind-set will produce results for the group.

We foresee the continued rise of home offices and women-owned businesses as Gen Y mothers try to balance work and family. Many of these companies will be technology-based because these young entrepreneurs believe they can provide an old service in a newer, faster way. The group mentality of this generation will likely produce a new business model that includes virtual employees and business partners. While companies once set up physical offices in multiple locations throughout the United States, you can expect to see companies that operate online with employees based in homes coast-to-coast to serve the needs of remote clients. A day may come when if a company has locations in Los Angeles, New York, and Miami, it truly means the company has an associate working from a home office. It's a solution that fits the lifestyle of these ambitious, confident, well-educated young adults.

GENERATION Ys AS MOTHERS

The trend toward traditionalism among members of Gen Y will become even clearer as they become mothers. Today, the oldest group of Generation Ys is the newest group of mothers and their numbers will continue to grow. Sociologists and researchers, using the opinions of today's tweens, teens, and college students, have predicted that these mothers will have more children at a younger age than any other generation in recent history. Sociologists predict younger marriages and larger families.

Gen Ys will be good mothers who demonstrate a great deal of confidence in this role. The practice they've had absorbing all forms of media at once has equipped them with multitasking skills like no other generation before them. Because they view education as a lifelong process, they will most likely instill the same values in their children. We believe that their return to religion and tradition will continue to fuel the homeschooling trend that has seen growth with Generation Xers. In 2003, about 1.1 million students were homeschooled, up from 850,000 in 1999. Thirty percent of parents opted for homeschooling to provide religious and moral instruction.[14]

The tight family bond that Generation Ys enjoyed as coddled children is likely to continue as they have their own children. They maintain close relationships with their mothers. Marketers can expect to see the grandmother's opinion and influence grow as these young mothers have children of their own. For this reason it is important for older brands not only to retain the loyalty of the Baby Boomer Mom Market but also to connect with new edgy messaging to their children, the Gen Y moms.

MARKETING TO GENERATION Y AS CONSUMERS

Marketers can lay the foundation to successful marketing to Gen Ys by focusing on their need for constant connectivity. They love talking to their friends and word of mouth is one of the most important influencers for this group. This generation has been speaking to each other since they were toddlers. No matter what medium they use, their messages are extremely important to each other. The objective in marketing to Gen Ys should not be blasting messages at them but rather creating a buzz that they want to participate in and share.

Like Gen Xers, they enjoy their individuality and they know marketers have been catering to this since they were young. Wooden puzzles cut in the letters of their name, storybooks whose main characters use their names, and CDs personalized with their favorite music have always been available to them. Online sites such as Amazon.com address them by their first names as if they were yet another member of the gang. This group wants a brand that meets its individualism. Thus, a brand must present the Gen Y mom with new fragrances, fresh colors, and packaging that fits her lifestyle needs. Remember, this is the generation that buys cars online, squeezes peanut butter out of a tube instead of using a spoon, and watches new releases in the car.

The desire to exhibit their individuality can also be seen in the contagious popularity of urban fashions. Trendy Gen Ys will take an off-the-shelf item, give it a twist, and suddenly it's an original creation that attracts attention. Grassroots interest will create the buzz and soon malls are filled with the newest trend. An example is the resurgence of rubber flip flops. Baby Boomer moms may refer to them as thongs. If you ask a Gen Y about her thongs you might get a strange look. These once $2 rubber shoes were worn only at the beach or in the backyard, and rarely in public. They were purchased in the aisles of grocery stores and drugstores. Today, young women parade the malls dressed in upscale brands such as Ralph Lauren or Coach while wearing rubber flip flops. Generation Y females don't follow any specific fashion rules. Thongs regained their popularity with the invention of the kitten heel and celebrities who sport them in magazines.

When Generation Ys make buying decisions, they draw on their mothers' message to them as children: they can be whatever they want to be. Today they have plenty of images to try on themselves, from Brittany to Eminem to Tiger. They process what they hear and see in advertising messages, decide what they want to be and what fits their lifestyles, and select the products that meet their needs. They don't want to know how long a product is going to last or how it performed in taste tests. They want to know how your product will help them become what they want to be. How is it relevant to their life? Instead of Nike's "Just Do It," Gen Ys respond to Gatorade's "Be Like Mike" campaign. For brands to connect with Gen Y, they must speak to Gen Ys' aspirations and visions of their ideal selves.

Although they are the best-educated population since the Generation Xers, no other population since the hippies has altered the English language as much. Hip-hop music has had a great deal to do with this. Gen Ys may most commonly be characterized by using such vernacular as "no problem," "bling bling," "dis," and "text" as a verb.

Generation Y has been bombarded with brand messages since they were babies. They know companies want their business. Since they were young, they have enjoyed special kid's meals, hotel camps, and kid clubs. Even a trip to the toy store is different for Gen Ys. Toys R Us now offers a shopping experience that might include riding Ferris wheels, making craft projects, or sampling the newest video games. Although these efforts have bred a generation that responds to multiple communication vehicles, it has also fueled distrust for brands. By the time they are legal adults, Gen Ys have experienced so much hype that they have become immune to standard brand messaging. Brands don't mean much to this cohort. Whether it's Coach, Tommy Hilfiger, Starbucks, Amazon, or Apple, this population owned brands that past generations categorized as luxury items and worked decades to afford. Gen Ys can be educated about brands, but they can't be sold. Like their predecessors, they have an astute awareness that technology can create incredible images and they approach advertising claims with skepticism.

In the following chapters we will examine in depth some of the most effective marketing initiatives for reaching Gen Y moms. However, we'd like to end with a thought that is worth mentioning more than once. To successfully reach this group, marketers, like employers, need to understand and find a niche that fits within the existing lifestyles of Gen Ys. Guerrilla marketing is one of the most effective approaches for doing this. Whether a Gen Y mom is in the kitchen preparing dinner for the family or playing on the floor with her toddler, it's important to her to be a part of the activity.

It's not too early for marketers to begin focusing on the emerging Mom Market being created by Generation Y females. As we've noted in this chapter, Gen Ys will be the largest group of spenders since the birth of Baby Boomer mothers. The good news for companies who have successfully marketed to the two preceding generations of moms is that they will find familiar qualities in Gen Y moms. These young mothers are conservative and ambitious like boomer moms but laid-back and relaxed in their approach like Gen X moms. And they share mothering attributes with Silver Birds. According to our research, like the most mature mothers before them, Gen Y moms believe themselves to be nurturing, strong, thoughtful, and generous. They are the most likely group of mothers to identify the composition of a family (single parent head of household, divorced family, gay family) to be one of the chief differences between their generation of mothers and the generation that preceded them.

Marketers will have to be nimble, however, to capture this market because they possess their own characteristics as a cohort. Gen Y moms are the most socioeconomic and ethnically diverse group in history. They appreciate differences and individuality and are very loyal to their peers. As mothers they are traditional in their parenting style and expect to have more children at a younger age. While dangers to children is the top factor Gen Y moms pointed to as making it harder to be a mom today, their optimism to create a better world for themselves and their children positions cause marketing as an effective strategy for companies who want to win the hearts of Gen Ys. Another important communication vehicle for marketers trying to create a meaningful relationship with this cohort will be technology. These women are used to exchanging ideas with friends and family via Instant Messaging, e-mail, and camera phones. Companies will need to speak to these consumers in more than language and with more than one medium. Word of mouth will be intensified as these moms share ideas even beyond their peers because Gen Y women like their mothers and other senior family members. The Mom Market is about to expand today as Generation Y women become the mothers of tomorrow. Wise marketers will begin to build brand loyalty today.

7

SILVER BIRDS,
GILDED WALLETS

Mommy's Having a Bad Day! Call 1-800-GRANDMA" reads a popular T-shirt design for babies. But these days, many children don't have to dial a phone to reach a grandparent, and when they do, they'll find one ready to do much more than bake the cliché cookies.

The American Association of Retired Persons (AARP) conducted a landmark grandparenting survey in 1999 and concluded that generations in today's society are significantly connected to each other despite a mobile society and busy lives.[1]

"The state of American grandparenting is strong," explains Gretchen Straw, Associate Research Director of the AARP Research Group. "The relationship with grandchildren is a rewarding one."

According to the survey, more than four in ten grandparents who are not caregivers and do not have grandchildren living with them see a grandchild at least weekly, and another 25 percent do so biweekly or monthly. Forty-five percent of grandparents talk weekly or more often via the telephone, and half say they sent or gave a greeting card to a grandchild in the past month.[2] Activities that grandparents and grandchildren share are wide-ranging, with eating together being the most popular (at home, 72 percent; out, 65 percent); roughly 40 percent to 50 percent say they watched a TV comedy together, watched an educational TV show, stayed overnight, shopped or browsed for clothes, engaged in exercise/sports, went to religious services, and/or rented a video.[3] The average grandparent spends about $500 a year on gifts and essentials for their grandkids and two in five spend up to $2,500 on them annually according to AARP.[4]

Grandparents today are a major force in grandchildren's lives, and as we'll explore in this chapter, Silver Bird grandparents are making their mark with grandchildren in ways their grandparents never envisioned.

THE NEW GRANDPARENT

While we discuss Baby Boomers separately in their own chapter, it is impossible to talk about Silver Bird grandmothers without addressing this cohort's influence on them. Baby Boomers influence every generation and life stage that they have touched, and as they move into the role of grandparent, they are making a large impact on perceptions and behavior associated with traditional grandmas and grampas.

"It's their demographic weight," says Michael Rybarski of Age Wave IMPACT, a California-based marketing firm. "Wherever the Baby Boom goes, it becomes the center of marketing opportunity in this country.[5] Boomers are healthier and more active. They fight aging and everything that aging represents . . . including the traditional image of a grandparent."

In the United States, 31 percent of adults—approximately 60 million Americans—are grandparents. Based on the fact that women outlive men, we can assume that more than half are grandmothers. And Baby Boomers represent a significant percentage of newly minted grandmothers.[6]

Allan and Kathryn Zullo penned their own how-to book, *The Nannas and the Papas: A Boomers' Guide to Grandparenting* (Andrews-McMeel, 1998), that provides insights about today's generation of grandparenting and is aimed at the younger, active grandparent set. "We're redefining the image of grandparents from the cookie-baking type to active grandparents who are in-line skating with their grandchildren," says Zullo. "We're very proactive in wanting to be part of our grandchildren's lives."

Within the newest group of grandmothers, we see the unique characteristics of Boomers who, in their youth, voiced antiwar sentiments, protested civil rights injustices, and demanded women's liberation and sexual freedom. Those who have or have had their own careers, who are both college-educated and independently minded, heavily populate this wave of women. They are intent on maintaining active, productive lives, yet are committed to rich relationships with their grandchildren.

Silver Birds, who focused on family for the majority of their adult lives and their time as mothers, are relishing the second opportunity to "mother" young children in new ways that help them feel useful and valued. The new tradition of grandmothers, regardless of whether they worked outside the home, are redefining the role of grandmothering today and, as a result, are faced with the balance issues often used to describe contemporary working mothers.

Boomers influenced Silver Bird moms by showing how they have fulfilled themselves both at home and in the workplace as their children achieved independence. Now many Silver Bird moms and grandmothers find themselves beginning new careers or adapting their lifestyles to make room for all the elements of life they most enjoy, on their own terms, during this later life stage. In the case of today's grandmothers, balance is the order of the day as necessitated by their need for self-fulfillment and the desire to be involved actively with their children's children.

"I never imagined I'd be doing a work and family balancing act at this age, but it's a much more conscious practice then when I was raising my own children" said Renee Baseman, 62, of Clearwater, Florida, a mental health counselor, wife of a practicing rabbi, mother of three adult daughters, and grandmother to five. "I feel fortunate to be so involved in my children's and grandchildren's lives and to also have a great marriage and do meaningful work. It's all come together at this time in my life." Playing multiple roles in her daily life causes her to juggle schedules and priorities, but she defines her lifestyle as well rounded and rewarding.

Jean Giles-Sims, Professor of Sociology at Texas Christian University and founder of Grandmother Connections, a lecture bureau and consulting firm that seeks to broaden the image of grandparenting to fit the new realities of the 21st century, has developed three profiles of today's grandmothers based on interviews with grandmothers of varied ethnic backgrounds, ages, and economic levels: traditional, empowered, and enlightened.

Traditional grandmothers give grandchildren stability, work to preserve family traditions and religious rituals, and focus on home-oriented contributions such as cooking. Often retired or working in limited capacities, they keep the family at the center of their lives, support traditional gender roles, and hold the "good old days" close to their hearts.

Empowered grandmothers enjoy social and economic freedom and handle careers on their own terms. Because they work, they have less time to devote to their grandchildren, but they use their resources to provide unique experiences and opportunities for these grandchildren, such as travel and extracurricular activities. They exemplify more modern gender and family roles and enjoy the chance to connect with their grandkids in ways they did not with their own children.

Enlightened grandmothers bridge traditional and modern roles by keeping family first, but also by encouraging children to be anything they want to be and exposing them to new ideas and experiences. They are often volunteers in the community and, while primarily defining themselves as wives and mothers, value exploration and demonstrate that anything is possible to achieve.

Age, stage of life, educational level, economic level, childhood influences, and desired involvement all play roles in which type of grandmother a Silver Bird is, but more of these grandparents are playing active roles in their grandchildren's lives than grandparents of previous generations.

Disney has been quick to recognize the more active role that grandparents are playing in the lives of their offspring. The 2004 campaign, Grand Gatherings, encouraged travel planners to book vacation packages with extended family members. Furthermore, they enhanced the Disney experience for these families by offering special Grand Gatherings that the entire group received for being a part of their group. Commercials and online information featured grandparents enjoying Disney features with grandchildren. This is a great example of creative marketing based on consumer trends and generational shifts.

Another company that has been successful in identifying opportunities associated with the youthful mind-set of Silver Birds is Tahitian Noni International. Zeroing in on the changing health focus of women over 40, Noni launched the Tahiti Trim® Plan 40™, a comprehensive weight-management program designed specifically for women over 40. The products combine hormones with the nutrients that the Silver Birds' aging bodies need.

In a discussion group in central New Jersey with mothers ranging in age from 45 to 65, mature grandmothers spoke of enjoying their grandchildren more than they felt they were able to enjoy their own children because they now had more time to be "in the moment." During their active parenting years, there was always laundry to be done, dinner to be made, or other household chores to finish. As grandmothers, they have learned to let lesser priorities go while they spend time with grandchildren. New Boomer grandmothers share this sentiment, but in a slightly different way.

While Silver Birds were originally focused on the home, Boomers were constantly out of the home, seeking rewards at work. Now as grandmothers, the Silver Birds can have what they feel they missed the first time around. "Women say that this is such a wonderful experience that they want for themselves—this time with the grandkids," says Dr. Giles-Sims. "They tell me it's just delicious." And the central importance of grandchildren is intensified by there simply being fewer to dote on. With Gen X and Gen Y daughters having children later, the opportunity for multiple grandchildren diminishes, so there is less pull in multiple directions for grandparents, and more opportunities for deeper relationship building.

Long-distance grandmothers explore the full possibilities of using technology to bring them closer to grandchildren, recording videos of them reading favorite books or using picture phones to send real-time images. Local grandmas maintain memberships to museums, libraries, and community centers to provide intellectual and physical stimulation for grandchildren and offer interesting experiences.

And as Boomers and Silver Birds explore the full range of grandma possibilities, you can forget about gray-haired grannies rocking away in their floral-designed living rooms. While it will eventually creep higher, the average age of first-time grandmothers today is a youthful 47 years old. With the current life expectancy at 76 years, a grandmother may spend 30 years or more in that role, making becoming a grandmother just another life stage instead of an end stage. As Boomer-filled Hollywood elevates the image of grandmothers, there will be more youthful, fun grandmas like Goldie Hawn out on the town with daughter Kate Hudson's baby boy, and Diane Keaton playing the attractive author in *Something's Gotta Give,* who ends the film with a romantic relationship, a successful career, and a new grandbaby to fill her days. As Silver Birds see their younger grandmother counterparts exploring new avenues of grand-parenting, they are eagerly following into uncharted territory.

GRANDPARENTS AS CAREGIVERS

It takes a village, or at least a grandmother, it would seem. Evolving beyond the traditional role of Saturday-night babysit-ter, grandparents are becoming a growing population of pri-mary caregivers. The full-time work ethic of boomer parents, the escalating rate of divorce, and the growing costs for child-care have spawned a cottage industry of grandmother nannies. In our research, interestingly, nearly three-fourths of Silver Birds indicated having at least one child under the age of 18 in the home, with an average of 1.8 children under the age of 18.

According to a U.S. Bureau of the Census survey, one in five preschoolers is supervised by a grandparent during at least part of the workweek.[7] That's even higher than the percentage of children under five who are sent to professional daycare centers or who are cared for by their fathers while their mothers work.

The 2000 census found that 5.8 million grandparents live with their grandchildren. Of those, 2.4 million, or 42 percent, say they are responsible for the child or children residing in the home.[8]

The 1997 national survey of families with children under age five reveals that 21 percent of preschoolers are in a grandpar-ent's care for at least some of the workweek, making grandpar-ents the leading childcare providers after stay-at-home mothers. In many of these cases, the grandmother caregiver role is vol-untary, and with more grandmothers maintaining jobs and volunteer positions or pursuing varied hobbies, the stereotypi-cal image of a grandma waiting at home for the chance to babysit and become involved in the grandchild's life has been turned around.[9]

It is equally likely today to see grandmothers taking their grandchildren along to activities already planned, such as volunteer projects or social events whenever possible. Instead of life revolving around a grandchild, today's grandma sees grandchildren as a complement to her already full life. But in some cases, the childcare is not voluntary, but necessary.

GRANDRAISING:
THE SECOND PARENTHOOD

In 1997, 3.9 million, or 5.5 percent, American children lived in households headed by a grandparent. This is a 76 percent increase over a 27-year period.[10] In 2001, according to a supplementary census population survey based on the 2000 census sample, 4.5 million grandparents maintained a household in which one or more of their grandchildren under age 18 lived with them.[11] Reasons offered for the increase include drug abuse among parents, teen pregnancy, divorce, rise of single-parent households, mental and physical illnesses, AIDS, crime, child abuse and neglect, and incarceration.

More than 2.4 million U.S. grandparents are responsible for most of the basic needs of one or more of the grandchildren they live with. Of these caregivers, 1.5 million are grandmothers responsible for raising one or more grandchildren.[12] Postings by these second-time parents on Internet message boards and weblogs illustrate the issues they face, from physical exhaustion to financial strain to loss of friends and the life they expected to have in their later years. While it may have been time to ride off into the sunset, these grandparents, while loving their grandchildren, find themselves isolated and frustrated with the primary caregiver roles they must take on when their kids—because of drug or other criminal problems, bad divorces, or abusive situations—cannot raise their own children. And while many of them are acting in parental roles, legally they are not able to adopt or be named guardians of these children. Lobbying and legislative efforts are well under way to address the legal issues associated with grandraising, as the number of grandparents in these roles continues to grow.[13]

PURCHASE POWER/ITEMS BOUGHT

The majority of grandparents today are over 60, and they are certainly the vocal majority, freely dispensing advice, discipline, love, and money. According to the AARP survey, mature grandparents with incomes of $75,000 or more spend $840 a year on items for grandchildren, and, as stated earlier, the average grandparent spends approximately $500 annually.[14] Clothing is by far the most frequently purchased item for grandchildren, followed by books. Significantly more Silver Bird respondents in our research mentioned media influence as a factor that makes mothering today harder. As a result, many Silver Bird grandmothers prefer purchasing toys with an educational element and often lean toward brands that have nostalgic value and remind them of their own childhoods, like LEGO and Matchbox. Products and brands that support worthwhile causes, benefit children's schools, or fund education through purchase percentages, such as Target and the Upromise program, influence buying decisions for this market.

Retailers that recognize grandmothers are also seeking time-saving opportunities and a desire to feel more youthful can capitalize on this trend to increase purchase amounts. For example, when a Silver Bird grandmother along with her Gen X daughter and toddler grandchild visited an Old Navy retail location, the primary goal was to buy back-to-school clothes for the grandchild. With clothes appropriate in size and style for each generation of the shopping party, all three found items they liked and bought.

Although spending is strong within the current grandparent market, estimated at $35 billion annually, it will most certainly skyrocket as more mature grandmothers, whose spending habits were irrevocably impacted by Depression-era childhoods, give way to aging Boomers wading into the grandparenting pool. Baby Boomers, known for their fondness for the good life, are among the wealthiest of the generations and intend to share that with their children's children. According to Packaged Facts, the estimated disposable income of Boomers over 50 is $1 trillion.[15]

In addition to buying toys, games, and clothing, Silver Bird grandmothers are also seeking experiences to buy, such as do-it-yourself kits for making jewelry or fossils, adventure travel, and materials to teach skills like woodworking or painting. These grandparents also favor solid wood toys and items of more simple construction, and are leading a resurgence of these types of toys with their demand for quality and long-lasting materials. The creation of a memory in the process of enjoying the purchase enhances value. Grandtravel, a Washington, D.C., based company that creates and leads educational travel itineraries for grandparents and grandchildren, is one example of the increasing popularity of experiential grandparent gifts. Peak season for their tours, which include domestic and international destinations, is during the summer when working parents are unable to spend a lot of time with children looking for things to do. Grandparents naturally step in. Some grandparents we have interviewed plan annual trips with grandchildren one-on-one, giving total attention to that child in a new place they can explore together. Although many gifts selected by today's grandmothers are intangible, grandparents today purchase more than 20 percent of the children's products sold, making grandparents an audience to be pursued and impossible to ignore.

SRI Consulting, a marketing services firm based in Menlo Park, California, has attempted to segment the grandparent population as a means of better defining and responding to its collective consumer behavior. SRI has established four behavior categories to describe most grandparents[16]:

1. *Traditionalists.* These consumers tend to be cautious, moralistic, and patriotic and is the largest group of today's grandparents. But because of the natural aging of this cohort, this population is waning. These consumers tend to be home-oriented and prefer tried-and-true brands.

2. *Makers.* This group of consumers tends to be more active than Traditionalists and is more likely to be independent and antiauthority.

3. *Achievers.* This group is more status-oriented and tends to value interpersonal relationships. As a result, its buying behavior often relies on peer influence.

4. *Thinkers.* These grandparents are driven by principles and by doing what's right. They are likely to acquire information and are thoughtful in their purchasing behavior. They research products before buying them. "The primary difference with the new wave of grandparents is they'll have a lot more resources—not just education and money, but also self-confidence, intellectualism, and global awareness—that will make them more open-minded and expressive in the marketplace," says SRI Senior Consultant Kathy Whitehouse. Thinker grandparents are more likely to consider the educational aspects when evaluating the purchase of a toy or other product.

While considering grandmothers as consumers, it's important to recognize how they do their purchasing. While many marketers believe that older consumers are more brand loyal, those over 45 are just as likely as younger consumers to experiment with or switch brands. More than 60 percent of consumers over age 45 say that quality is the most important factor when choosing a brand.[17] Also, it's outdated to think grandmothers aren't shopping online. According to the Senate Committee on Technology, about half of the consumers over age 50 have personal computers, and 70 percent of them have Internet access. More than 90 percent of PC owners have shopped online and 78 percent have made purchases.

Discounts provided by organizations such as AARP and AAA enable grandparents to spend on items or experiences while enjoying savings, such as hotels that allow children to stay free when sharing a room with a grandparent and gift card savings at retailers like Toys R Us.

Companies can leverage this trend by offering special promotions focused on experiences they can share with their grandchildren such as movies and other amusements. You must also remember that to gain their awareness you need to publicize these discounts in areas where they gather information such as condo newsletters, clubhouse bulletins, and community center communications.

FUNDING EDUCATION

A group discussion among grandmothers in Tampa, Florida, ages 59 through 68 with a total of 15 grandchildren, underscored just how seriously grandmothers take their perceived responsibility for the care, feeding, and enrichment of their grandchildren. In addition to funding the more traditional gifts and outings, these women spoke openly about their roles in providing for their grandchildren's schooling because their children weren't able to accommodate the cost of private school tuition. The grandmothers felt it was essential. "If we want our grandchildren to be in particular programs, and it's cost-prohibitive for our kids, we just pay for it. It's too important to us," said Susan Telli, a grandmother of eight.

Indeed, according to a 2002 AARP survey, more than half of grandparents help pay for their grandchildren's educations. Forty-five percent help pay for living expenses and 25 percent contribute to their grandchild's dental or medical costs.[18] This trend presents a great opportunity for financial institutions to increase their product lines and offer to include services that make it easy for a grandparent to make these contributions.

According to the AARP grandparenting survey, 12 percent of grandparents who made a purchase within the past 12 months financially supported school tuition or daycare. Eleven percent of grandparents funded camp programs. Many grandparents anecdotally told us that they like to pay for the "extras" like dance lessons, language classes, or sports uniforms so that grandchildren can participate in the extracurricular activities they want without straining the parents' wallets.

GRANDMOTHER POWER

Grandmothers are everywhere. From the delivery room when her grandchildren are born to the pediatrician's office for the annual physicals, grandmothers are making their presence known. Their approval is critical to marketers when they are helping to choose cribs or cough medicine or the right school or activity for their grandchild. They are a critical target audience when seeking to capture the Mom Market or influence child purchases.

And, in case you still need an illustration of a true Silver Bird grandmother today, take Grace Cline as an example. At 74, she is a fixture in Frenchtown, Montana, where she was born and raised. She reared three children in the small rural town of about 800 residents and now regularly interacts with several of her nine grandchildren who still live nearby. Recently, she supervised the reconstruction of her home following a fire that destroyed all her belongings. She was surprised to have been invited to deliver the commencement address at the graduation ceremonies of the local eighth grade class, but accepted. Her speech extolled the virtues of maintaining a positive attitude in the face of adversity and using life's challenges to grow and learn. She was stunned and impressed that she was able to keep the attention of the students in the audience, who listened attentively without fidgeting. She believes she taught them something important and useful that day.

As her name suggests, Grace epitomizes the attitudes and behavior of the Greatest Generation and is eager to stay connected to the youth in her life, whether grandchildren or members of the local Little League teams. She knows that she can make a difference with many of the children in her community by sharing her knowledge and her time. "When I was growing up, you had to improvise and do without some things, but it was great because you did things as a family," Grace said. "There are so many grandparents either raising or helping to raise their grandchildren today and serving as role models."

Grace shows no signs of slowing down, and neither does the rest of the Silver Bird grandmother cohort. With a desire to share experiences and solidify relationships with their grandchildren, these consumers are receptive to messages that will help them create memorable times together.

For marketers, Silver Birds represent expanded opportunities and secondary market segments for products traditionally purchased by mothers for use with their own children. Grandmothers today are purchasing items such as infant products, college savings funds, video cameras, and even piano lessons on behalf of their daughters and sons for their grandchildren. Companies who want to capture this spending should recognize the youthfulness of today's grandmother and focus on the experiences she is sharing with subsequent generations. As these women grasp for immortality, nothing can be more powerful to them than knowing that their purchases are in some way laying the foundation for future generations by creating a gift that may, indeed, last forever.

8

MESSAGES FOR MOMS

Words and images create the core of a successful marketing plan aimed at mothers. These two elements, regardless of their application to a mom's life, establish the basis of the relationships they establish with others. Words serve as the outward expression of their feelings and emotions. Whether it's a simple "I love you" between a mother and her toddler or a stern "Don't do that again!" between a mom and her teen, the words mothers use are important tools of expression. An action that forms the images she sees creates the impressions she will later apply to a person, product, or brand. Think back to your teenage years. Remember when your mom saw one of your best buddies hanging out with someone who was smoking outside a convenience store and suddenly by association she became leery of your friend? You found it difficult to understand why she would no longer allow you to hang out with that friend. Well, it's time to finally understand your mother. The reason for her response was that moms associate actions they see with images they form in their minds. Her subsequent behavior is based on whether those preconceived notions are positive or negative. Your friend might never have touched a cigarette in his life, but the image of what could happen if he smoked, or offered one to you, produces an overwhelmingly negative image. She reacts to protect her child. As a marketer, the words and images you use to communicate your marketing messages can produce the same reaction in mothers today. The only difference is that instead of selecting friends for her children, she's choosing the brands and products she introduces to them.

Relationships represent one of the most valued aspects of a mother's life, whether it's the relationship she has with her child or with peer groups as we see with Gen Ys. The words you use to lay the foundation can mean a long and lucrative relationship for your company.

Moms like to be addressed by marketers in the same manner that they speak with their friends. This means chatting about topics that are relevant and real to moms. Our research has identified themes that resonate conversations between moms and we will examine each in depth within this chapter. A word of caution to copywriters before they scrap copy that is currently on the table: Although you want to communicate in a way that says "We get you" to a mom, you don't want to sound patronizing in your attempt to join her group of friends. In other words, don't use every newly discovered slang expression without putting meaning behind the words—like a New Yorker trying to use "Ya'll" in south Georgia. The execution would be there but it would lack authenticity. Perceptive women can see right through this. And it's not just about the words; it's how a mom uses and associates the words with emotions. For instance, a client recently asked Maria for her opinion about ads it was preparing to release. The ad copy repeatedly used the word *guilt* four times in two sentences. Moms will tell you that although guilt is a big issue at times of their day, they do not want to be reminded of it. In fact, when moms talk about guilt they rarely use the word—even in conversations with their friends. The first question Maria asked was the gender of the copywriter. We apologize in advance and mean no disrespect to our male readers but the answer was a young, childless male. He and the brand manager had pages and pages of research that supported their strategy that moms felt guilt. They wanted to present moms with a solution to the guilt acquired when life gets in the way of spending time with their children. What these men missed, however, was how moms communicate their guilt to others. It's rarely by using the actual word. Often it's masked in other terms such as "I've felt torn between" or "My life seems unbalanced" or "There's a lot coming at me right now." When moms speak of guilt to another mom it's in terms of the effect it has on their lives. The company's lack of understanding of this almost cost it a large ad budget that would have produced little in sales and perhaps would have deterred moms from using its brand altogether.

These brand managers are not alone. In fact, we surveyed mothers on their opinions of advertising and found that many marketers are missing their target. Only 20 percent of mothers said that advertisers were doing a good job connecting with mothers. Another 70 percent said that marketers are not focusing on moms in their advertising and 30 percent said that they see ads that offend them. This means that great opportunities exist for marketers who connect with mothers using the right words and images.

One of the most consistent elements of marketing to moms that we've found over the years is the common touch points of mothers. Five themes form the foundation of all meaningful conversations with mothers: time, value, family enrichment, solutions, and family health. We will examine how a marketer can use these topics to create a meaningful dialogue with mothers. Additionally, several other areas are emerging as important focal points for advertisers. The first centers on family diet.

With media attention on child obesity and marketers scrambling to convey healthy choices to consumers, we thought it was important to address. Second, we will examine the dynamic line between focusing your marketing message on a mom's child and speaking to her as a woman. Our most recent research has uncovered several insights on the effectiveness of these two focal points in your words and images. Let's first turn our attention to the one commodity every mother lacks: time.

THE TIME TECHNIQUE

Every mother searches for a "25th hour" in her day. In fact, this is the expression used to describe the need for more time. Few moms, regardless of the number or age of their children, feel like they have enough time in their day to do all the things they desire or are required to do. Mothers—whether Boomers, Xers, or Ys—want products and services that save them time. As we've already discussed, these moms perceive time as having great value and their use of it varies. Boomer mothers will pay more for a product that saves them time. They are the most likely of all mothers to spend more money for convenience or to acquire time. Their position in life allows them to solve problems with money because they have more disposable income than their younger cohorts. It's not uncommon to hear a Baby Boomer mom say, "I'll pay a little more if it ultimately will save me time." These mothers are also more likely to be in the workforce, which takes them away from their children for a period of time each day. They place an elevated value on products and services that allow them to spend additional time with their families or maximize their efforts in balancing work and family. They will weigh the cost of the product against their hourly pay to justify the extra cents. For instance, one mom recently described her buying decisions in this manner: "If I can save 30 minutes of driving across town by spending an extra $2, it's worth it to me if you consider my time is normally worth $50 an hour and I can be home before my children go to bed." In her mind, she was gaining time with her family and saving $48 in her personal time. Gen Xers and Gen Ys have been utilizing technology to help them manage time since they were young. They expect companies to recognize that saving time means providing them with extra hours for leisure activities or family fun. Their use of the time you save them is quantified in a different manner but valued just as much.

The most successful use of time in your messaging to moms is to place value on how they will spend the time you save them. It's not enough anymore just to say "We'll save you time" because young technology-savvy mothers know how to find time-saving solutions online or by utilizing their wireless tools. For example, we recently evaluated a print advertisement for an online shopping destination that carried the headline, "We'll save you an hour but how you choose to spend it is up to you." The ad pictured a young mother with her child in a park. It was a great use of the time theme. The ad allowed moms to put their own value on the time they saved using the service. Then it went one step further and gave moms a visual that was realistic to their lifestyles and aspirations as mothers. Although we are discussing the words you use, it's also important to remember that the credibility of your messaging is built on your actions. You can convey your time-saving attributes by offering services that reinforce your desire to help moms save time. Such services might include online ordering, customer-service call centers, and purchase tracking systems to reinforce this message. These extensions of your brand promise are particularly important to younger mothers who expect to interact with you through multiple channels and who also expect you to be sincere with them as mothers and as women.

Because we've mentioned the importance of value, let's examine this area next as an effective theme in your advertising messages.

THE VALUE OF VALUE

Women share the thrill of getting a good deal, but to them value means much more than paying the cheapest price for a product. Moms want good value, but the quality of the product and the fulfillment of the brand promise contribute to the equation. Call it Mom Math: quality + performance + benefits = value. This perception of value varies within each demographical generation of mothers.

Baby Boomer moms demonstrate a concept known as trading up and down. Their higher income levels and amounts of discretionary funds allow them to pick and choose what items they splurge on. These moms will carry a $300 Kate Spade diaper bag but shop at Target for their children's clothes. Determining where your product or service falls in their trading hierarchy is important to increasing sales. Successful marketers can elevate the position on a mom's hierarchy by gaining an understanding of her potential shopping behavior and combining this with actual customer data. When a mother makes a purchase, the value a company provides her contributes to her position as the family CFO and in this role she wants to feel like a hero. The boomer mom wants to demonstrate her financial independence by making wise purchasing decisions that produce great experiences for her family. These women will spend hours on travel sites seeking the best price for the memorable experiences they desire to create for their children. Low-cost travel providers have a great opportunity to tap the wallets of boomer moms.

Generation Xers see value as a means to enhance the lifestyles they desire for their families. Because many of these women are choosing to either stay in the home or remain single, price matters to the overall cash flow of their families. They realize that financial stability is as important to the secure environment they desire for their children as an involved parent. Price comparison and special values enable a Gen X mom to take ownership of her family's structure. Additionally, these young moms know how to utilize the Internet to find value. They are comfortable printing discounts, surfing for freebies, and conducting price comparisons online.

Generation Y women have had little to do with being frugal because they've been the object of their boomer parents' prosperity. Their perception of value is based more on the word of friends and whether the product produces the result they seek. However, this is not a generation of waste. Their conservative ideas translate into educated buying decisions weighted on the quality of the product and the position it gives them among peers.

Quality, in fact, influences the purchasing decision of all mothers. The weight of this element actually circles back to their appreciation of time. Mothers invest so much time researching a product before purchasing it because they want the brand to deliver on its promises so they don't have to reinvest their time searching for a replacement. Even if they pay less, they still expect a certain level of quality in the product. Marketers can stress quality when highlighting the benefits the brand delivers to mothers. You can communicate the concepts of value, quality, and benefits through imagery as well as words.

FAMILY ENRICHMENT

Family enrichment is another theme that produces effective messaging to mothers. This broad topic includes learning, loving, and raising confident children. Boomer mothers invested in child enrichment as a way to compensate for the time they were away from their children in the workplace. They spent money on expensive cultural art lessons, language schools, personal athletic coaches, and private schools to allow their offspring to reap the benefits from the fruits of their labor. The result was twofold. First, they fueled a tidal wave of developmental products and services that pushed children to excel beyond their age and abilities. The push for success that boomer moms demonstrated on the corporate ladder turned to their children. Today, moms overwhelmingly say they see other mothers who push their children to achieve more at an earlier age. In a recent research project we conducted, 75 percent of mothers said they witnessed this behavior within their peer group. Ironically, only 30 percent admitted that they mimic these actions with their own children. The second outcome was that the children who were the object of boomer moms' overscheduled parenting style grew up to redefine family enrichment.

Although today's younger mothers want to lay a foundation for their children that gives them a head start to future success, these moms have a greater appreciation for the emotional growth of their children. They want to be involved in creating enriching moments with their children. They want to understand child development, how to maximize it, and how to make it a joint venture. In the same study, we asked mothers if they could know one thing about their babies, what would it be? Sixty-two percent of them said they would like to know what their children are experiencing while learning new skills. Companies who can give moms this insight and offer products that allow them to share in the growing experience will be successful. LeapFrog, maker of educational toys, has been successful in connecting with moms in this manner. It offers specific age-related toys that create a learning experience for both child and mother. Additionally, its retail destinations are organized so that mothers can see the natural progression in learning and the toys associated with it. Knowledge is important and considered cool to Generation Y. Whether it's something new to teach her child or a new way to teach her about her child, a Gen Y mom is likely to appreciate the intellectual point of connection. In this light, LeapFrog's tagline, "Learn Something New Every Day," is positioned well to appeal to younger mothers.

Education is an important touch point for mothers of all generations, whether they see it as a means to prepare children at an earlier age for the future or as a means to provide their children with more than past generations did. Marketers have been quick to cash in on this common parenting concern by attaching educational promises to their products regardless of any validated research. The rush to tag the word *educational* onto toys, foods, videos, and services is being saturated. Moms are wise to the fact that not every product that touts learning can help her breed the next Einstein. In fact, there is a move to allow children to enjoy play just for what it is, play, and to accept the fact that not every aspect of play has to be managed with educational benefits. An undercurrent in articles and discussions in the mom world suggests that traditional play, which doesn't include computers, voice detection, and audio tools, is the best type of learning experience for their children. Companies need to be cautious in overplaying the educational benefits of their products or services, particularly if they are unconfirmed or unrealistic.

SOLUTIONS

Moms are the greatest problem solvers in history. Perhaps they haven't signed treaties to end wars, but they have mastered the art of negotiating whose turn it is to use the blue PS2 (PlayStation 2) controller. They've found a way to make a big purple dinosaur sing and dance and a way to deliver online auctions to millions around the globe. Whether they are Sheryl Leach, creator of Barney, the dinosaur, or Meg Whitman, CEO of eBay, or the mom down the street, moms are always solving problems and creating solutions. If you are a company that understands your market, these moms want you to join them in their quest for solutions. For this reason, solution-based messaging is quite effective in the Mom Market. Creative marketers should identify universal challenges that mothers face and present solutions to them. Here's an example of a problem faced by moms when it's time to travel with their children: how to pack snacks without taking along the entire bag of chips, dried fruit, or cookies. The answer: use Ziploc bags. In one of the best marketing messages we've seen lately, Ziploc bags ran a sweepstakes, giving away a family vacation; its copy offered this advice: "When you leave, keep your food fresh by using Ziploc bags." What this idea did was to marry a basic everyday challenge of a mother with an easy answer. Most important, it told the mom that Ziploc got it. It made the consumer feel like Ziploc had spied in her kitchen. There's a lot more opportunities for similar types of question-and-answer marketing. What mom doesn't pack a roll of paper towels in the van when it's time for a summer road trip? A similar promotion could involve a drive destination or hotel change and Bounty paper towels. And what if mothers all over the country knew that the secret to removing playground sand from a child's feet was to sprinkle baby powder on them and brush with one's hand. Magically, it's gone. I bet every mother in America would carry Johnson & Johnson Baby Powder to the park. Tie in the message with a day-at-the-park giveaway that might include bikes, picnic supplies, and a tote with baby powder to remove the sand.

One way to determine where your brand fits into the lives of solution-oriented mothers is to ask moms how they use your product. You may find that they are using it in a way that solves a problem that has nothing to do with the benefits or features of your product. For instance, a large number of moms in the Sun Belt use frozen juice boxes as ice packs in their children's lunch boxes. The benefit to these mothers is that they can provide their children with healthy drinks while keeping their sandwiches cool as well. Makers of juice boxes should test their products in the freezer to determine additional messaging opportunities. As two mothers who live in the South, we can report that only certain brands use adhesive on their straws that is strong enough to keep them attached after being frozen. No mother wants her child to be without a straw for his or her juice at lunchtime. This is a great opportunity for juice brands to tout the freezer-friendly features of their boxes with solution-based messaging.

FAMILY HEALTH

Few things rank higher on a mother's list of concerns than the health of her family. Messages that highlight the health benefits of a product or service are effective in marketing campaigns. It's important to ensure, however, that the benefits are well documented and credible. When it comes to the health of her family, a mother will consult numerous sources to validate a product's promises. The behavior of mothers when it comes to the health of their children is very interesting. Although they respect the recommendation of their doctors the first time they use medical products, moms tell us that they turn to the Internet and magazines for updates on the latest medical news.

The focus of mothers on the health of their families goes beyond just medical implications. Mothers include body image and dietary requirements that contribute to the overall well-being of herself and her children. Although mothers of all generations have been faced with maintaining daily vitamin intake and fighting the common cold, one of the greatest health-related changes involves body image and the diet that attributes to the physical growth of their families.

BODY IMAGE

Baby Boomers are feeling younger than ever. Thanks to movies like *Something's Gotta Give*, the perception of age has changed. No longer is 40 the downhill turning point for women—and companies that have recognized this fact have prospered. The success of Old Navy can be attributed to the hip, fountain-of-youth appearance it provides to Baby Boomer moms. What Old Navy also offers Baby Boomer mothers is the opportunity to shop in the same place as their tween and teen daughters and find clothes that they can wear as well.

These women do not want to be depicted in ads as older women. They respond best to images of youthful, active-looking mothers. The value of body image lies not so much in what they actually look like but the aspirational impressions they hold in their minds.

Josephine Chaus, chairwoman and CEO of Bernard Chaus, Inc., identifies changes in the way moms are dressing: "There has been a casualization of fashion—from personal to business life. No longer is it necessary to be perfectly adorned, head to toe. This is a reflection of a few factors: a more comfortable and relaxed universal attitude toward self, the democratization of luxury (women are mixing and matching high-priced items with more affordable fashion), and a lifestyle that requires that one be fluid and flexible."

Chaus says that younger women are expressing their personalities and confidence in the clothes they are selecting to wear.

"They enjoy experimenting with colors, fabrics, and silhouettes—dabbling in the more-buttoned-up fashion of yesterday via vintage clothing. Taking fashion cues from past generations and reinterpreting them for today is popular with this crowd. Still, the casualization that has permeated fashion for the past decade will probably not disappear. I believe that mixing casual and formal wear will produce an exciting result—the customization and personalization of fashion on a larger scale."

The change of attitude toward body image is best illustrated by the changing style of maternity wear. As expectant mothers, Generation Xers and Gen Ys are demonstrating their self-confidence in their body images by wearing tight-fitting maternity clothes. In fact, Gen Xers are the first generation of expectant mothers to wear clothing that accentuates their tummies. Thus, it should come as no surprise that the first designer of fitted maternity wear was a Gen Xer herself. When Liz Lange looked at the clothing offered for expectant mothers in the late 1990s, she realized there was room for attire that celebrated the changing body style during pregnancy.

"I think that there has been a revolution in the maternity fashion world and women simply refuse to hide behind big tented dresses that make them look like amorphous blobs," says Lange, whose Liz Lange Maternity line is carried at Target stores. "Women shouldn't have to take nine months off of fashionable dressing. Today's moms simply can't. They work through their pregnancies often in high-powered jobs, have a social life, and travel. Fitted sexy, but appropriate, clothing is a reflection of all that."

The self-image of Generation Y women has also been shaped by an increased awareness of obesity and the media attention of elective cosmetic surgery. The many choices these women have regarding how they look and dress has sparked a proliferation of new industries and marketing opportunities. Not only does this generation have more "good-looking" fat-clothes options than any cohort before, but they are opting for breast implants before they graduate from high school. They can bleach their teeth, pierce every body part imaginable, and inject collagen to produce fuller lips. The Internet allows them to design outfits and customize fashions. Their heightened sense of fashion is an opening for marketers to focus on the look and feel of their products, particularly if the product has a designer name attached to it. For instance, Eddie Bauer car seats or Lands' End diaper bags would appeal to these moms. Focus on the functionality at the same time that you appeal to moms' strong sense of fashion.

FAMILY DIET

One of the greatest challenges for all mothers is feeding their families. The struggle starts from birth when she faces the great debate between breast-feeding or using formula to feed her baby. Later it continues as she attempts to get a toddler to eat anything other than french fries and chicken tenders. As her family grows, she is challenged with fixing creative school lunches and quick meals for dinner that can be eaten on the run. It comes as no surprise that more than 60 percent of moms we surveyed say they do not know what they are cooking for dinner at 4 PM. One company we worked with saw an increase in retention by offering to-go meals for its working parents. As if meal planning weren't a big enough challenge, today's moms are now faced with media pressure to control their children's diet to combat child obesity. The pressure on moms to produce healthy, quick, and easy meals that taste good is immense. Companies who present a solution to this challenge will reap great returns on their investment. However, the attempt to meet the meal planning and dietary needs of a mother must be sincere. You cannot profess to be a healthy alternative unless you indeed offer multiple healthy choices. The opportunities in this area go beyond listing "Fat Free" or "Sugarless" on your labels because moms know it's not realistic to expect their children to eat healthy every time they consume food. Your messaging has to send a fresh idea that makes it easy for moms to make healthy choices for their families. A good example of this is Pepsico's new Smart Spot Smart Choices program that puts a product identifier on healthier products within the Pepsico family. The ad introduces the program by calling it a "helpful little short-cut to a healthier life." There are several great features of the program and the advertisement. First, the bright green label helps moms quickly pick out healthier choices for their fami-lies. Kids are going to eat chips, but which ones are better than the others? Pepsico takes the work out of determining this for moms. Second, the ad features lifestyle snapshots along with experiences that are relevant to mothers. One box says, "Giggle like you mean it," while another touts, "Race your kids to the front door." The images are happy and feature moms and kids with Pepsico products. The campaign is right on target for Gen X and Y moms who want you to speak to them as a peers.

BABY TALK

For years, marketers have put the child at the forefront of their messaging to mothers. If the company is selling a stroller, it will focus its message on the comfortable seat positions for baby rather than the stroller's easy-to-fold feature for mom. While this is an effective means of marketing to moms, its use-fulness decreases as the ages of their children increase. We as-sume that marketers take this approach because they have always done so. We feel, however, that it's worthwhile to explain why this approach works today primarily with Gen X and Gen Y mothers. These women tend to be first-time mothers and moth-ers of today's youngest children. In the hierarchy of values, there is nothing a mother values more than her baby. She will set aside her own identity and the needs that coincide with that as a woman to focus on her child's needs. So messaging that focuses on the benefits to the babies works well with these mothers because they will do anything to give their offspring the very best. This strategy, however, begins to lose effectiveness as their children grow and obtain independence. During this process, a mom begins to take back some of her identity. There is a new interest to return to her roots and resume her old pleasures. You can see this by examining the older segment of Baby Boomer mothers. These women no longer are martyrs of motherhood. They are indulging in spa treatments, taking on physical challenges such as marathon running or cross-country skiing, and partaking in girls' weekend shopping sprees. As their children grow, mothers regain their identities as women.

Marketers also use the children to market to mothers by winning the hearts of their children. Although moms are not fans of pester power or the nag factor, they will make purchases

Ways to Market to Moms by Empowering Their Children

1. New products that are wholesome for kids and desirable to moms
2. Advertising targeted to kids that moms see and find appealing
3. Products at retail that kids want and moms want for them
4. Promotions that energize kids and delight moms
5. Prizes and premiums that are fun for kids and acceptable to moms
6. Contests with prizes that reward the entire family
7. In-school programs that deliver learning to kids and benefits to the school or community
8. Internet marketing that enriches kids and inspires moms' permission
9. Place-based programs that cater to kids and make the visit easier and more enjoyable for moms
10. Family marketing that embraces mom and kid together

List compiled by Paul Kurnit, founder and president of KidShop, a youth-focused marketing communications company.

based on a desire to please their children. They will also purchase a product to ensure that their children are accepted by their peers. We leave youth marketing to youth marketers, but felt it was important to recognize this practice by some companies.

MOM BONDING

Marketers who grow with a mother will grow sales. Moms have told us that they are more likely to use a product that changes as their lifestyles move through the multiple phases of motherhood. Remember, moms want to know that you "get" them, and recognizing the stages they experience will do that. This strategy works well for a company that offers a broad base of consumer products such as Procter & Gamble, Unilever, and Johnson & Johnson. In fact, the latter recently produced a Sunday insert that did an excellent job of taking a mom from No More Tears shampoo to lotion for her own legs. It's extremely important for marketers to remember that moms are women with children. Although a mom always carries the responsibility of being a mother with her, she never relinquishes her identity as a woman. Marketers who recognize her multiple roles will be successful winning her heart.

So how do you find the right message to utilize in your marketing to mothers? Go back to the heart of your product. Define your core and be straight about it. Moms want you to be sincere and credible no matter what you are focusing on. Determine what truly makes your brand unique and describe how it can meet the needs and lifestyle of your target customer. Convey your message in a friendly fashion that speaks to her as a peer rather than as an authority figure. Present solutions that contribute to the big picture. Moms will focus on end results so it is very important to let them know up front why the information you are presenting is valuable to them. They like to control the outcome of their efforts and are very confident in obtaining the results they seek to find. Today's moms do not like to be spoon-fed or force-fed and, in fact, they resent this approach. A marketer would never want to tell Gen X moms that they must use this product to achieve the result. A more welcomed approach would be to deliver your message with useful information that allows the mom to grow in knowledge but leads her to your desired behavior as well. Be honest because the worse thing you can do is to try to deceive technology-savvy mothers. Messages of rebellionism will not work with Gen Y moms because they have such an admiration for their parents. Deliver your message so that moms connect with your product. Take the message to them wherever they congregate: malls, playgrounds, and learning centers, and allow them to encounter your message in multiple ways.

Now that we've examined the messages that connect with mothers, it's time to put them into action.

9

REACHING THE RIGHT MOMS THE WRITE WAY

There are many ways to deliver your message to the Mom Market. If you are to take away any one marketing strategy from this book, we hope it will be that you must deliver your message to moms through multiple channels. To be successful in winning the hearts of the Mom Market, you must carry on a meaningful conversation with her in numerous venues. She needs to hear from you on air, find resources with you in print, and interact with you online. A mom wants to find you in the places she frequents at the times that she needs you but also in places that she doesn't expect to find you. The latter will communicate to her that you are perceptive to her needs and truly understand her lifestyle as a mom, woman, and business professional. Just as this new generation of mothers is integrating various aspects of their lives into their roles as mothers, they want you to follow them in their lifestyles. The bottom line is that to be successful in the Mom Market, marketers must consider all forms of marketing initiatives as part of an effective strategy. Print communications in the form of advertising or custom pieces are just one aspect of the overall plan. We are going to examine some of the most popular forms of printed delivery mediums.

DIRECT MAIL

Direct mail has undergone many changes in the past decade. What once was mainly distribution of catalogs, postcards, and brochures has now become a channel of circulation for content and interactive elements such as compact discs (CDs) and software. Although the best-designed direct-mail pieces can be effective in creating a dialogue with mothers, rising postage costs has required some marketers to reexamine their strategies. Traditional means of direct mail such as flyers and postcards are less effective in the Mom Market than more original content-based pieces such as magalogs, a combination of magazine and catalog, and custom publications. The latter will be discussed later in this chapter. A mom's mailbox is a crowded landscape. If she gets beyond the numerous credit card offers she receives, she finds little time to ponder unsolicited mail during her busy day. The nature of her multitasking abilities enables her to sort mail as she is stirring macaroni on the stove and quizzing a child on his spelling words. Chances are your postcard is reaching her when her attention is more focused on multiple tasks than on your marketing message. The only exception is direct mail that is extremely timely and tied to a lifestyle event such as camp registration, back to school, or religious events. Although postcards and brochures are not one of our favorite marketing strategies, here are a few tips that can raise your rate of response in the Mom Market.

First, find the right list. You must specifically identify who you want to target with your message. Hopefully, you will be able to apply some of the insights of the preceding chapters to segment your target audience. All too often we watch marketers cast a net over mothers in the hopes of catching the attention of at least part of them. When the direct-mail piece does not produce the results the marketers desire, they fault the messaging or creative departments rather than their mailing list. Using a bad list fuels the adage "Garbage in, garbage out." An inadequately defined mailing list is simply a poor use of marketing funds. The second tip we have for direct mail also coincides with your audience. Make certain your message is timely and relevant to the mothers receiving it. There's no use sending a formula offer to a mom with teenagers. This seems like an extreme example, but we assure you it happens every day. The numbers games that marketers have used for years in direct mail will not work in the Mom Market and can even backfire if a mother perceives your irrelevance as insincerity. This is how negative buzz begins among moms. For the best results when sending direct-mail pieces to moms, marketers need to deliver a very personal message that is relevant to the place she is in in her motherhood.

The best direct-mail marketing tools in the Mom Market are catalogs, magalogs, and content-based custom publications. Later in this chapter we will take a more detailed look at what makes each of these communication vehicles effective. First, we will examine the most popular form of written communication in the Mom Market—magazines.

MAGAZINES

Nearly every research project we conduct for clients includes some digging into where moms find product information. Although 80 percent of moms tell us they go online to do their consumer research, magazines serve as the second most important source of information. Interestingly, publications such as *Child, Parenting,* and *Parents* rank higher than pediatricians when it comes to finding medical updates and trends. On average, even the busiest moms say they read 4.1 magazines a month, with at least two of these titles delivered to their mailboxes. In addition, moms tell us that they are more likely to purchase a product they read about in the content of a magazine article than by seeing it in a stand-alone ad. We find no disparity in moms' magazine readership based on their generation or the ages of their children. Moms like magazines. Delia Passi, CEO of Medelia Communications and former publisher of *Working Mother* and *Working Woman* magazines, describes a mom's devotion to print publications in this way: "Moms value the relationship they have with their favorite magazine because it provides them a wonderful environment in which they can escape for a while yet find solutions and tips that they can later apply to their real life." Says Passi, "It's almost like a quick trip away, justified by the learning experience they bring back with them."

What may differ among mothers are the titles they are reading. As you might suspect, expectant mothers are reading *American Baby, Fit Pregnancy,* and *Pregnancy* magazines and then moving into *Parenting, Parents,* and *Child* after they give birth. As her children's development becomes less of her focus during the school years, she returns to her own pleasures and enjoys *SELF, People, Woman's Day,* and *Glamour.* We note two emerging trends in moms and magazine readership. One is a move toward magazines that allow her to share the content with her child. With the return to traditional motherhood, we see magazines such as Disney's *Family Fun* and Scholastic's *Parent & Child* well poised to capture the attention of a growing market of mothers who are looking for activities to share with their children. Second is the growing popularity of niche content such as organic foods, education, and religious lifestyles. We feel this is attributed to the personalization that Generation Xers and Gen Ys desire in their everyday life. In addition, time-starved mothers are looking for faster ways to get to the content they can apply to their life. Therefore, they are seeking one-stop sourcing for the topics that are relevant to their needs. A working mother doesn't want to flip through an entire magazine looking for tidbits of work and life balance information in a women's title but rather wants to read a magazine devoted to the subject such as *Working Mother* or our own *Today's BlueSuitMom* magazine.

The changes that moms are fueling in the magazine world not only are touching the types of publications and content that magazines deliver but the type of print advertising in them. Mary Beth Wright, publisher of Disney's *Family Fun* magazine and a veteran in the magazine industry, sees an evolution in advertisers: "Many companies such as computer hardware and software, digital technologies, credit cards, and home improvement who traditionally targeted men have begun to embrace the spending power of moms by positioning their brands in magazines such as *Family Fun*." She adds that their ads are successful when their creative is synergetic with the "real world of moms [that] includes a family member and provides her with solutions."

This approach to connecting with moms has created a new look inside the magazines. The black-and-white line between editorial and advertising has become gray as marketers have looked for ways to rise above the clutter, and declining advertising revenues have forced publishers to create new types of advertising packages. The outcome of these challenges has been to integrate content into advertising. Although it's a concept that works well for connecting with moms, it's a strategy that is being hotly debated. We'll allow those who have an interest in journalistic integrity and publishing policies to reach a middle ground while we discuss why it's a strategy that works in the Mom Market. As long as the content is valid and credible, moms don't mind how the information appears on the page. They are smart enough to know that a company purchased the space but many view it as just another way for the brand to deliver their content. They are more likely to read the ad and for the most part appreciate the tips and solutions many advertisers are now providing as their hook.

We've already mentioned the research we have to support content over ads on our effectiveness meter, so if done well, the strategy works in the Mom Market. We want to stress, however, that your content must be credible. Moms are huge fans of second opinions. If they try to validate your information with another source and find that it is not credible, your brand loses credibility as well. Today's moms want to trust the brands they buy. Unfortunately, a mom's second opinion is only one Google away on the Internet.

THE NEW PRINT AD

Magazine ads are changing for the good when it comes to marketing to moms. Instead of screaming features to the reader, they are providing solutions and benefits through content. The approach works well for information-thirsty moms looking for new ways to perform old tasks like painting a bedroom or cooking pasta. Smart marketers have simultaneously recognized that the same valuable content they stored on their Web sites could be just as valuable in print. This assumption is correct for reasons beyond just the value of the content. It's an important strategy because Gen X and Gen Y moms want to interact with your brand through multiple channels in much the same way they interact with their friends. They want to dialogue with you in different ways at different times. Supplying these moms with information in print ads is just another channel of communication.

Let's look at a few examples of companies that successfully integrate content into advertising in print. Home Depot has recently begun adding how-to content to ads that feature home improvement merchandise. They successfully bond with female readers by empowering them with the know-how to use the merchandise and the products that Home Depot sells. It comes as no surprise to marketing professionals that the mastermind behind this approach is John Costello, Home Depot's EVP of Marketing, who in a prior career developed "the Softer Side of Sears."

McDonald's is also running content-based ads. The print campaign showing up in parenting publications gives tips for moms on a number of lifestyle situations. The latest one offers moms solutions for carpeting a family room. A good approach to moms is "We understand your challenges and we are part of your team." The feeling that they are associating with peers is appealing to Gen X and Gen Y moms.

Marketers can still be effective in print advertising without incorporating content. Strong solution-based messaging still works well in attracting the eyes of money-spending moms. The best way to see what works and what doesn't is to grab a stack of magazines and start turning the pages.

HITS AND MISSES

We believe there's no better way to learn about print advertising than to flip through pages and pages of it. It's an activity that we like to do weekly. There's nothing like a stack of monthly women's magazines or the Sunday newspaper to see who's attracting moms and who's driving them away. A few hours will help you understand why 30 percent of moms say they see ads that offend them, according to research conducted for *Marketing to Moms*.

Let's take a look at some ads that hit the mark with moms. It's no surprise that we start with one of America's biggest print advertisers. Fortunately for McDonald's, it is currently spending its money well at attracting mothers. The company is running an ad in parenting publications for McDonald's new line of salads with the headline, "Now Mummy has her Yummy." The graphic includes a picture of a mother and her child and a salad. We like the picture of the mom because she's dressed in hip boots, but what we like most is McDonald's message. It acknowledges what moms have known for years. Moms will cave to their children's pleas for Happy Meals but will wait to eat later until they can have a healthier choice for themselves. In this ad McDonald's says that it understands what moms have been feeling and has made changes to give them the chance to eat as well. This is a great message that speaks to a universal behavior in the Mom Market.

Another company that has highlighted a universal mom challenge and presented a solution to it in an ad is Dodge. This car company is one of the few that consistently produces the right messages for moms. A couple of years ago, the company ran an ad that read, "Who was the stupid guy who coined the expression Stay-at-Home Mom?" The copy spoke directly to busy moms who often feel unrecognized for the job it takes to run a household. This year its ad speaks to moms but this time addresses their quest for more storage space in the garage. The new ad focuses on a foldable rear seat in the Dodge Caravan. Instead of just saying, "Hey, look we have it," the tagline says, "We've found a better place than your garage for your minivan seats." Recognizing that a mom had to find a place to store the rear seat when she removed it, Dodge not only came up with a way to solve that problem but a creative way to communicate the new feature to her. Keep up the good work, Dodge.

MasterCard has mastered the Mom Market in its new priceless print ad in parenting publications. With a young girl standing in goggles and swimsuit, the ad, which partners MasterCard with Kmart, says, "No floaties, no fear: priceless." MasterCard is right, there are some things that money can't buy and one of them is when your child can swim. Kmart and MasterCard recognize that in the stages of development for a mom, it's an important accomplishment for her child to swim.

Now for a look at a few companies who miss the mark while marketing to moms. In the spirit of moms being forgiving, we'll keep the brand names secret in hopes that they'll improve in the future.

In a very expensive mistake, a car company purchased four full-page ads in a parenting magazine. The series of pages focused on various types of people and the vehicles that fit their personalities. The first ad, which featured a business-woman, was termed "The Wildly Rational Woman." There was no indication from her appearance or the other graphics in the picture that she had children and the car paired with her was a sedan. The second page featured "The Infinitely Fertile Man," a thirtysomething guy with four cribs in the background. As expected, he was featured with a minivan. The third page turned the spotlight on another thirtysomething man known as "The See-Every-Monument Dad" and an SUV. The final page of advertising explained the three preceding pages of advertising with copy that said, "The People with So Many Needs . . . The Company with So Many Choices." It was a great concept but poorly executed. Where was the mom in the campaign?

This ad campaign missed the target for a number of reasons. First, it failed to link the mother with the ads by helping her picture herself, either literally or figuratively, with the product. Remember, moms want to see people like themselves in ads, in commercials, and online. It's about reality. Second, the infinitely fertile man positions the male contribution in reproduction in a somewhat negative, unequal manner. Confident women of the new millennium understand that they can't become moms without men, but they don't want to think they need men. Additionally, with the rising number of single mothers, it is a dangerous approach to feature two traditional fathers in one ad series. The company can be perceived as exclusively aimed at single mothers. Although our research shows that most moms aspire to have a nuclear family, they know that it may not be their reality. This ad campaign would have been better executed if the car company had presented different types of moms and the cars that fit their individual needs.

It always hurts to see a first-timer fail, but, unfortunately, that's the case with a new print advertiser and its campaign. A well-known maternity apparel retailer took a step into print advertising. The message the company was trying to convey was that pregnant women could look beautiful wearing its clothes. It's a great message because moms will tell you that body image is one thing that can suffer when being pregnant. The illustrations it used to convey this message, however, missed the mark. The ads pictured a very pregnant mother walking by an outdoor café wearing the retailer's clothes. In the background sitting at a table is a young man and his girlfriend. The young man is gawking at the pregnant woman as his girlfriend is giving him a dirty look. With a generation of mothers so focused on creating a secure family for their children, introducing any level of "unfaithful in men" is a major no-no.

Although women love the attention of men, they don't necessarily like it from a man who is apparently taken by another woman—particularly with Generation Y women who have such a strong loyalty to friends. These women would never appreciate having a friend's guy gawk at them. In contrast, another maternity-wear company used the same message but featured a pregnant woman almost in the same scene minus the feuding couple and added a tagline, "Style that will keep you out and about for all the nine months." This is essentially the same message with better execution.

Magazine advertising can be expensive for companies with small marketing budgets. To these marketers we suggest testing

---

Smaller Niche Magazines to Consider

- Adoptive Families
- Twins
- Moment
- Vegetarian Times
- Christian Parenting Today
- American Girl
- Home School Digest
- Home Education Learning Magazine
- Early Childhood Today
- The Soccer Source
- Mom's Business Magazine
- Today's BlueSuitMom
- Catholic Parent
- Sportingkid

your ads in smaller niche publications. They can be just as effective as the big books but with smaller price tags. Though not as slick, these magazines often have a very loyal group of readers who patronize advertisers in appreciation for their shared interest.

CUSTOM PUBLICATIONS

In an attempt to capitalize on the popularity of magazines, companies are investing in custom publications as a means to deliver valuable content to the Mom Market. The strategy is extremely popular with companies targeting expectant or new mothers. For example, Enfamil produces a publication called *Family Beginnings* that features month-by-month developmental information for new moms. This is a good strategy because new mothers read so much to find the right products for their babies. Although it's a good way to connect with your market, this can be an expensive endeavor for marketers with smaller budgets. Printing costs and postage add a large price tag to custom publications unless you have creative distribution channels.

One way to divert costs of a custom publication is to find partners. Song, Delta's low-fare provider, has partnered with American Express. They produced a piece called *Talk about Song in the City: Guide to Stylish Travel*. Because New York is one of Song's major destinations, the pocket-size book features restaurant reviews, tour suggestions, and a shopping guide. The American Express logo can be found on the cover and throughout the book. Song distributes the book on all flights in and out of New York, which places American Express outside its normal advertising reach. This strategy works well because it integrates both brands into the lifestyles of moms traveling to the Big Apple. Both Song and American Express are touching customers at a time when the information is timely, relevant, and useful.

MAGALOGS

A new form of direct mail that falls under the category of custom publications is magalogs, a combination of magazine and catalog. Retailers such as Abercrombie & Fitch and Neiman Marcus are blazing the trail in delivering content while presenting merchandise to consumers. Abercrombie's book, *A & F Quarterly*, contains paid advertising by other brands that seek to tap the retailer's customer base. Information-seeking consumers seem to accept the paid content that retailers are presenting in their magalogs. In fact, it's almost appealing to young mothers who like to interact with brands through different channels of communication. We expect to see magalogs continue to grow as marketers see positive responses from the Mom Market.

CATALOGS

Companies who remain faithful to a product-focused format still have the opportunity to tap the wallets of mothers. Revenue generated from catalog sales to mothers is big business. According to the National Mail Order Association (http://www.nmoa.org), mail order–related sales in the United States exceeded $1.7 trillion in 2000. In fact, 69 percent of consumers buy from catalogs, and moms are a large part of that number. The dollars spent on toys, games, and children's products through mail order totaled more than $2 billion during the same year. Almost 13 percent of mail-order apparel sales are in children's clothing and more than 3.3 million people purchased baby accessories via mail order. Catalog consumers age 26 to 35 spend the most on children's items while mothers age 36 to 45 come in a close second. All this means sales for marketers who successfully win the hearts of the Mom Market.[1]

Catalogs targeting mothers, like print advertising, should contain designs that allow mothers to picture themselves or members of their families in the product. Many children's retailers use large pictures of smiling children. This visual works well because mothers love to see their children smiling. *CWD, Children's Wear Digest,* differentiated itself from other Spring 2002 catalogs by using a collage of smiling children. This technique not only set its cover apart but also allowed it to quickly show moms the variety of sizes, shapes, and styles the catalog contained. A good strategy for speaking to the time restraints of a busy mother says to the consumer, "We know you are busy and we took that into consideration." It also lets the mother determine that the catalog is relevant to her, whether she has a toddler or a preteen, because all are pictured on the cover.

Another ingredient necessary for catalogs that want to succeed with mothers is the call to action. The best catalogs make it easy for a mother to order their products by offering a variety of ways to buy. These can range from fax to online e-commerce. A mother doesn't have time to look for a phone number in the fine print, so place your phone number and Web site address in the same location on every page of your catalog so when a mother dog-ears a page—folds down a page in a triangular shape to mark the page—with desired merchandise, she has everything she needs on that page to order the product.

In a catalog or any direct-mail piece, you can establish trust by clearly displaying return policies, forms of payment, shipping information, gift-wrapping details, and customer guarantees. The more information you provide your customer, the less she will suspect you are hiding from them. It is also important to disclose your privacy policy. Even if you don't intend to sell your customer list, tell your readers. This will go a long way to making them feel like they are doing business in a safe environment.

We believe there will always be room for traditional catalogs in the Mom Market. The changes that will occur, however, will be in how a company's catalog interacts with its other marketing initiatives such as its Web site and its retail location. Mothers who want retailers to adapt to their lifestyles will require companies to allow moms to move from one purchasing channel to another. For instance, the most innovative retailers will provide moms with catalogs to preselect merchandise before they order it online after the kids go to bed. Then the retailers will allow moms to pick up their orders at their local stores the next day while running errands. Because this is the way moms integrate technology into their brick-and-mortar lives, this is how successful marketers must design their marketing efforts. The messages and channels must all flow together so moms can adapt your brand to their reality.

Some catalogers have taken the cues of moms and created niche books specifically targeted at lifestyle behavior. Perhaps one of the best executed is Pottery Barn Kids and Pottery Barn Teen catalogs. The traditionally kitchen-focused retailer recognized the trend in home decorating and honed in on moms designing kids' rooms. They presented a one-stop shopping solution for mothers who, prior to receiving the new catalog, spent hours going from one store to another searching for themed accessories. Now when junior wants a football-themed bedroom, his mother can find everything from doorknobs to light switches to sheets in that motif. In fact, today's moms often use the catalogs as a way to involve their children in the decision-making process. These niche catalogs are effective in appealing to a generation of women who place high value on personalization and fashion.

The most successful catalogs will integrate interactive elements into their content. This can be accomplished by linking the pages of your book to your Web site to allow moms to take the next step into your brand. For instance, a fully integrated marketing plan may provide a mother with a colorful mail catalog presenting a variety of merchandise. However, it may promote an online design center that allows the reader to personalize the look of the product she is ordering. Your Web site could offer a 360-degree view of the shirt a mother is considering or show it on a model whose body shape is similar to her body. Mothers, particularly younger moms, want to be able to interact through various channels with you and tend to be more loyal to your brand when they can.

NEWSPAPERS

It was not by accident that newspapers landed at the end of this chapter. Only 19 percent of mothers tell us that they check newspapers when looking for products and information for their family. This statistic surely is disappointing for newspaper publishers, but it gives them a great deal of opportunity—and incentive—to be creative in the future. One exception to the attention moms give to newspapers can be found in the food section and Sunday inserts. We find that value-conscious mothers will comb food ads for price comparisons and take the time to read Sunday FSIs. Newspapers can improve on readership in the Mom Market by focusing on three areas: content delivery, layout, and reader know-how.

Moms must believe that there is some benefit in spending their overbooked time reading the newspaper. They want the same solutions, ideas, tips, and advice they can find online, and publishers have to figure out how to deliver that type of content on a daily basis within the editorial standards of their publications. Articles have to be short and relevant to moms' lifestyles. Young moms can't view the paper as something their fathers read at the dinner table or after dinner. Content must be laid out in a manner that is intuitive to a woman yet simple to navigate. The challenge for editors is to know what lifestyle tasks link together. For instance, moms who are searching for weekend activities for their children are most likely also going to be meal planning for the same Saturday and Sunday. How can the newspaper link the two to present her with an easy solution? Perhaps the answer is to position an easy-to-cook meal idea next to the calendar listings—and to please the advertising department, sell the adjoining space to a food advertiser.

Finally, newspapers have to educate moms on how to use the newspaper to save time and money. Papers are filled with great tools for moms, from coupons to classified ads, but newspapers have always fallen short by not educating their consumers on how to actually use these tools. Instead, newspapers tout their news coverage and features rather than the how-tos of using the paper. There is a huge opportunity to reposition this marketing medium as more mothers spend more time in the home.

CIRCULATION AND DISTRIBUTION

Marketers who want to successfully penetrate the Mom Market should think of creative means of distribution. Not only will this approach help you break through the clutter of traditional means of communication, but it can also put your content in front of a mother when it's relevant. You can produce the best messages and promotional materials, but if they don't reach their intended audience at the relevant time, they will fail in their mission. Getting your written materials in the right place becomes even more important with a new generation of mothers who expect to interact with the brands they use at all stages and places of their day. Your brand execution will be tested as mothers test your understanding of their behavior. If you really *get* them, then they expect you to be where they are, offering solutions along the way. Marketers must think past the traditional channels of distribution. Magazines need to find circulation in addition to subscriptions and newsstands, while direct mailers must find ways to expand their distribution beyond the post box.

The best way to discover new distribution channels is to track your customer throughout her day. For instance, if she is an expectant mother, she likely is spending time at a local hospital attending childbirthing classes, shopping for nursery items, or visiting the obstetrician's office once a month. By fully under-standing her behavior, you will identify places that present the opportunity to get in front of her with your printed messages. When we launched *Today's BlueSuitMom* magazine, we knew that we could not jump from start-up to newsstand so we walked in the shoes of our target market—working mothers. What we found was that mothers relied heavily on their employers' work and family or human resources departments for help on juggling careers and families. We also discovered that HR departments with shrinking budgets were looking for resources to fill the needs of their working mothers.

Our magazine provided a solution for both employer and employee. Rather than utilizing traditional means of circula-tion, we sent bulk shipments to work and family departments. Additionally, we went directly to our bluesuitmoms.com audi-ence with an offer to supply the magazine to their peers if they signed up their companies for bulk shipments. Within one day, our circulation went from 0 to 20,000. As we've discussed ear-lier, partnerships are good ways to put your message in a place where you would ordinarily not appear. This holds true for cir-culation and distribution as well.

As you can see, a smorgasbord of printable opportunities is available for marketers to use to deliver their messages. Content is the most important element of any printed marketing mes-sages, whether it's how-to lists or solution-based ad copy. Once you have selected the one print strategy that best fits your bud-get and target audience, delivery is the most important consid-eration. It must be timely and relevant to your target's lifestyle. You must be creative in its distribution and get your marketing materials in front of your moms wherever you find them. Look beyond traditional means of circulation to places that moms frequent, such as her car, parks, and learning centers. Finally, the most successful marketing teams will create integrated strate-gies that allow moms to react when and how it best suits their style, whether its online, on the phone, or through the mail. A multifaceted marketing strategy will not only allow you to capture her next purchase but retain her as a loyal customer.

10

GETTING MOMS BUZZING THROUGH PUBLIC RELATIONS

Public relations is one of the most effective means for connecting with moms. The advantage to this marketing art form is that savvy consuming mothers are more skeptical about claims made through paid advertising. That's not to suggest that advertising is not an excellent marketing form, but public relations provides the platform to communicate messages and build relationships with consumers without the extraordinary time limitations of a ten-word headline, a 60-second radio spot, or a 30-second television commercial. Imagine trying to educate moms about an issue, like the need to save for college, or a new category of products, such as Dryel, a do-it-yourself dry cleaning product, without the benefit of editorial-based media.

Yet, it is amazing how many marketers forget to include a public relations campaign in their communication or marketing strategy. It surprises us how often we are called to a company to discuss marketing to moms and find that the public relations manager is missing from the meeting. In most cases, everyone from the research manager to the packaging team will be present but no representative from corporate communications or public relations. Today's marketing professionals are not to blame for this oversight. Organizational charts within corporate America have long kept the two disciplines separate, choosing to focus the public relations department on investor relations or corporate media.

Two years ago we worked with one Fortune 100 company whose public relations department had never been involved in any communication other than with investor relations. We created a marketing strategy for a seasonal product that included a public relations effort. The three-month public relations initiative aimed at women with children consumers, resulted in news features in seven major markets, four million online impressions, more than three hours of radio interviews, and mentions in 50+ local newspapers. Needless to say, the public relations department of this company has changed its focus a great deal in the past two years and PR representatives attend all marketing strategy meetings within the company.

The public relations discipline is going through a revolution and we like to think that moms had something to do with initiating a change in our industry. Companies who have integrated public relations into their marketing strategy to moms have realized that public relations is one of the most effective and cost-efficient means to connect with the market. For your company to deploy a successful public relations campaign, it's important to understand why public relations is so effective in reaching the Mom Market.

Moms have a thirst for learning. During no other time in a woman's life—other than planning for her wedding—does she consume more information. From the time that blue line appears in her home pregnancy test, she's on a quest for knowledge. Research with our friends at StorkAvenue, the largest printable birth announcement company in the United States, tells us that expectant mothers begin searching for baby names as soon as their first trimester. Bob Hunter, CEO of StorkAvenue, says expectant mothers start requesting birth announcement catalogs as early as their tenth week of pregnancy. Boomer moms found their information in books and magazines. Today, Generation X and Generation Y mothers-to-be comb the Internet for products, advice, day-by-day accounts of their body changes, and online chats with other moms-to-be. They compare everything from belly size to fetal positions—on message boards, in chat rooms, and with instant messages.

A well-executed public relations campaign can put you in the middle of these online conversations. The emergence of the Internet together with Gen X's and Gen Y's dependency on it for information has broadened the reach of public relations. The days of a single press release to announce a new product are gone. The World Wide Web with millions of searchable destinations now offers public relations professionals just as many channels of distribution. The Internet can turn a paper release into a multimedia source of valuable information for prospective clients that has an incredibly long shelf life. And, it speaks a language that Gen X and Gen Y moms speak, a very important part of conducting a meaningful conversation. Your online message can take the form of content, expert advice by a spokesperson, radio interviews, instant messages, interactive surveys, and newsletter announcements. This will become increasingly important with Gen Y moms who demand multiple points of contact with a brand.

Offline, moms tell us that they seek updates on products and news on health issues from magazine content. In two different surveys in 2004 we asked moms for their offline source of information. The response was the same in both projects. More than 80 percent of moms said they turn to magazines for the latest news and information. This number was higher than the figures for their mothers, newspapers, or even their pediatricians. In fact, 65 percent said they were more likely to purchase a product because of an article they read in a magazine than an ad they saw in the same publication. This is great news for public relations professionals. It means that your efforts will translate into sales. Our research also shows that even the busiest mom reads 4.1 magazines a month with at least two titles being delivered to her home.

In their book, *The Fall of Advertising and the Rise of Public Relations,* best-selling authors and marketing consultants Al and Laura Ries give a boost to the public relations industry with straightforward advice about the heightened importance of non-paid media.[1] They discuss how advertising isn't the brand builder it once was and that public relations is now carrying that load. According to a write-up about the book on Amazon.com, "A closer look at the history of the most successful modern brands shows this to be true. In fact, an astonishing number of brands, including Palm, Starbucks, The Body Shop, Wal-Mart, Red Bull, and ZARA, have been built with virtually no advertising."

Moms have definitely given new meaning to public relations. It's up to you to get the conversation going by developing a strong plan that supports your marketing strategy. The most important goal of any public relations plan focused on moms is to create a buzz because of the intensified nature of word of mouth among mothers. The best way to accomplish this, particularly with Gen X and Gen Y moms, is to give them information that they can spread. Moms love to show other moms that they know something new or some way that is just a little bit better than another mom's.

Bridget Brennan, of The Zeno Groups' Speaking Female, describes a woman's eagerness to spread the word: "Women love telling people about new things they've discovered. Sharing news about everything from a new celebrity lipstick to a really good cough syrup is fundamental to women's conversations. If they can find your product first, in the context of a newspaper story, magazine article, Web site, or television program, it gives them the fuel they need to pass on the information through the method every marketer covets: word of mouth," says Brennan. "Women simply love to pass on news. The role of public relations is to put your product in the news. "

Bill Southard, president and CEO of Southard Communications, reminds us that the proliferation of media outlets over the past 20 years makes it even more important to hone your message and identify nontraditional avenues for your communications. Southard underscored this concept with an example of how a well-orchestrated program can be maximized by providing mothers with an opportunity to experience a brand. In the fall of 2004, the manufacturers of Etch A Sketch established a National Creativity Day, encouraging mothers to bring out the best creative talents of their children. Moms and kids were given an opportunity to try an electronic drawing product. The success of this campaign was attributed to the experiential nature of the campaign, rather than to a more static straightforward media relations push.

MOMS WANT TO FEEL SMART

Empower moms with knowledge. This newfound trinket of information can be a helpful hint, a new statistic, a creative idea, a new solution, or a funny story. For boomer moms the touch point is more likely to be a solution to an everyday challenge, while the Gen Xers and Gen Ys will appreciate a creative idea or statistic that allows them to use their intellect in applying it to their lifestyle.

Although you are likely to start with a press release once you decide on your campaign's focus, connecting to moms will call for some new approaches to public relations. Your initiative should include some type of interactive element that puts you in the world of your audience. Consider partnering with a Web site that moms frequent to conduct an online survey. This will give you a point of entry into the conversations already taking place within their virtual community. Later when you announce your results in press release form, you will have already established credibility with your target audience.

A leading public relations firm was tasked with launching a new Procter & Gamble spray-on laundry product—Downy Wrinkle Releaser—that removes wrinkles from clothes without ironing. Because of the unique nature of the product, one of the key challenges was to educate moms about Downy Wrinkle Releaser and quickly insinuate it into consumers' existing laundry habits. The firm used an interesting twist, though, and made college students the target audience; it put the spotlight on moms with messages that suggested these grown-up kids can learn to do laundry as well as their mothers, with program T-shirts emblazoned with the theme "Because Mom doesn't do your laundry any more." A key to the program was the strategy for college students to "push" the products to their own moms. The highly integrated program included Wrinkle Free demonstrations, a contest, activities designed to inspire influencers to spread the word about the product, and media relations. The campaign was measured through awareness surveys, consumer feedback cards, Web site traffic, and contest participation and either met or exceeded objectives on all fronts.

Another consideration might be to align your brand with a peer from their group. Remember how important friends are to Gen Xers and Gen Ys? Ask someone they trust who has an established audience within the market to be your spokesperson. It appears far less self-serving if someone else is delivering your message, particularly within generations of skeptical consumers. Save your connection to celebrities for another project; moms would rather learn from other moms. In a recent survey we did for a baby product company, we asked moms if they would rather get information from a celebrity mom or an experienced mom like themselves. Sixty-seven percent said they would more likely turn to a peer mom. Remember when selecting a voice for your company that real is important to moms. They want to be able to relate to the mother they see or hear in your campaign. Although Katie Couric and Kelly Ripa are popular moms, few moms believe they share the same challenges on a daily basis. You should also give moms a way to apply your knowledge to their lifestyles. If you discover that hundreds of moms hate to cook hamburgers because of splattering grease, provide ideas on how to cook without the grease. Finally, when you have all these ingredients assembled, distribute the information in as many forms and venues as possible. Although the traditional channels such as radio, television, and print will serve you well, remember not to forget online magazines, Internet radio and satellite tours, e-newsletters, and minisites.

We share a passion for public relations and interestingly have experienced it both from a development side and as the object of several campaigns. We felt that we'd deliver the most value to you by sharing some of the most effective campaigns we've been a part of.

Now let's look at a successful public relations campaign from the inside out—from Maria's view as a spokesperson for Office Depot. It's not often that a company has an expert in marketing to moms as its voice to moms, but such is the case for America's largest office supply company. For the past three years, Maria has been Office Depot's Family Organizational Expert. The role was the brainchild of Brian Levine, Director of Public Relations, when he launched the first Back-to-School public relations campaign for Office Depot. The company realized that women make up 80 percent of the foot traffic into their stores and by capturing more of the back-to-school purchases of these women, it could increase sales.

The public relations campaign began with a survey of mothers on their back-to-school shopping behaviors and the challenges they experienced preparing their families for the first bell. The results showed that 78 percent of parents waited until the last minute to buy school supplies, which caused 89 percent of them to feel disorganized. Armed with this information, Office Depot then created a list of ways moms could prepare their families for a successful school year. One of those suggestions was building a home communications center as a means of keeping everyone's schedules posted in one place, along with in and out boxes for mom to organize all the papers that needed to be signed and returned to school. Utilizing Maria as its spokesperson, Office Depot booked radio, television, and print interviews for Maria so she could communicate to moms all the great ways they could overcome their feelings of disorganization created by the back-to-school season. As part of every interview, Maria described to moms how they could build their own home communications stations. In true "Martha Stewart" style, Maria made the solutions sound easy and adaptable to any lifestyle. In addition, Maria's tips for family organization were distributed to numerous Web sites, featured in electronic newsletters, and posted as content on Officedepot.com. The results of the campaign were noticed not only in millions of media exposures but in sales as well. Although we cannot disclose exact numbers, sales for the products featured in the home communications center increased more than any other back-to-school product that season—a true sign that moms heard the message.

The campaign was successful in connecting with moms because it delivered the information through a series of different mediums, it contained useful and valuable information, and it offered a solution to a universal problem. Additionally, Office Depot used a peer who was trusted by her audience.

One good public relations campaign will not win you a place in the hearts of moms nor will it earn you a larger expense budget. Just as you must build credibility with your audience by delivering on your product promises, you must earn the trust of your internal customers as well. The latter will likely want you to deliver to the bottom line in sales, increased brand awareness, or some other benchmark. It's important to establish accountable measures of success while developing your public relations plan. You will want to be able to show how your efforts made a difference to the overall results of the marketing strategy. It's the way you earn credibility with those same executives who have been drawing organizational charts with PR alienated from marketing. Prove to internal teams that public relations deserves a seat at the table by setting benchmarks to illustrate your results. If you want to impact sales, make sure you include specific product mentions in press releases and spokesperson comments. Count everything from media impressions to print inches and give them a value based on what your company would have spent for that time. Make it meaningful to those who count so that public relations becomes an important part of marketing to mothers.

Creating a buzz about your product is more important than ever as a new generation of connected moms grows in number. Quench their thirst for knowledge by creating a public relations plan that establishes your brand as an expert resource on mom topics. Use the media to help spread your message, and supply them with easy-to-print lists of solutions, tips, and advice for moms. Then find a voice in virtual communities that can carry your message to her followers and keep the conversation going. Successful marketers will consider public relations campaigns part of their overall marketing strategy. Remember to be your own best publicist by communicating the results of your public relations efforts to key executives. We are certain that if you execute a strong message through multiple channels, you will find that public relations will provide you with the greatest returns on investments in the Mom Market.

11

CONNECTING WITH MOMS THROUGH BRAND EXPERIENCES

Some people believe that actions speak louder than words, and that may hold true in the Mom Market with one exception: Actions are equally important as words. Moms search for brands they can trust with the health and welfare of their families, and these brands must reinforce their words with actions to earn moms' trust. It's time to take the messages developed and delivered in print and bring them to life. This is important to a new generation of moms who appreciate reality and the choices it presents to them. Today's electronic environment presents marketers with a variety of communication outlets, from cable programming to radio. Although electronic mediums enable you to mass-market your brand to moms, we cannot forget the human-related marketing venues that put your messages into motion: special events, cause marketing, the retail experience. They all play a part in communicating a cohesive marketing message to moms. We even included in this chapter a discussion on packaging and product development because it carries your brand promises from shopping cart to kitchen counter. Moms are on the move so it's time to put your marketing message on the road with them. It's time to gas up the Suburban and get going.

TELEVISION

Television has long been a favorite of many big-budgeted brands. The idea of reaching millions of viewers at one time is extremely appealing to marketers. Up until the expansion of its audience with the cable networks, television offered a limited means of targeting specific markets. Advertisers could select programming that skewed to a certain age bracket or a particular gender, but for the most part there is a reason it's called mass marketing. Because of the broadly cast net that television ads throw, marketers have been reluctant to target specific segments of women such as moms for fear of offending childless women, single females, or fathers in general. Instead, advertisers stopped short in their messages aimed directly at the Mom Market even if the ads show a mom and children. It's no wonder that moms tell us that television commercials are rarely designed to speak to them. Fortunately, cable networks opened up a new form of electronic advertising that allows marketers to narrow their scope. Networks such as Lifetime TV, HGTV, Oxygen, and Discovery Health provide advertisers with new options to reach moms. These networks not only are increasing visibility for brands by putting target ads in front of their audiences, but they are creating new forms of advertising through segment sponsorships and product placement. This strategy works well in the Mom Market because it allows mothers to interact with the products and the personalities who represent them on several planes. Let's look at the success of TLC's *Trading Spaces* and its host Paige Davis. Moms looking for decorating tips bond with Paige through the television show just as they would with a girlfriend. She empowers them with home re-decorating ideas and exposes them to Home Depot products while painting a room or designing a kitchen. A commercial for Benjamin Moore paints touts its durability in a kid's room. While buying diapers at Target, the mom picks up a copy of one of Paige's books to read after the kids go to bed. She makes a trip to Home Depot for the paint she needs to finish her nursery and while in line at the register flips through a magazine with TLC articles in it. In no fewer than three moments in her week, she interacts with TLC's programming and the brands it repre-sents. This fully integrated messaging speaks to her lifestyle and allows her to interact with the brand beyond her couch.

We believe that television programs will eventually travel the road that retail catalogs did in creating magalogs. We see tele-vision of the future being produced by innovative marketers who will control not only product placements but content as well. Our research shows that consumers eager for information will turn a blind eye to companies who produce their own shows as a way to empower viewers with solutions. We foresee a day when Wal-Mart produces its own lifestyle show and sells ad space to the same consumer product companies that compete for its shelf space. Wal-Mart will present products that can be ordered online at special prices while the show is airing. Then to drive traffic into their stores, it will offer next-day pickup of online orders at a concierge desk. Online coupons good at the time of pickup would encourage shoppers to move from the concierge desk to the aisle of the store. Wal-Mart has already taken the first step in this direction by producing its custom magazine, *For Her.* Custom programming would allow Wal-Mart or any other innovative retailer that turned to this type of integrated marketing to control not only the spending channels of moms but their customer experience as well. It's the optimum lifestyle marketing initiative.

RADIO

We believe one of the most untapped marketing opportunities for reaching mothers is radio. When you consider how many hours a mother is in her vehicle and the extensive link between Generation Y and music, radio presents a natural means of communication between marketers and moms. Yet think about today's programming as it relates to the interests of mothers. AM stations blast sports talk shows and political fodder at her, and her choices of female programming are considerably limited, with the controversial Dr. Laura as the main headliner. Turning the dial to FM, she finds her tween's favorite music programmed into the dial or Radio Disney blaring toddler chants. Ironically, she spends more time in the vehicle than either of the target audiences of these AM and FM selections.

It is estimated that more than 60 percent of all radio listeners are female and that more than 50 percent of all listening takes place in cars.[1] To further support our theory, the Surface Transportation Policy Project, a coalition of organizations interested in transportation policy, reports that single mothers spend 75 minutes a day driving, while married women with children drive 66 minutes a day. Eight out of ten women are radio listeners.[2] The best part about radio is that moms can listen while at work, in the car, at home, or at the park. Moms have access to radio virtually anywhere they go during the day.

Radio offers two opportunities for marketers. First is the traditional 15- to 60-second spot. These spots are great for time-sensitive messages with quick calls to action. Here is an example of an untapped opportunity for a smart food product or quick-serve meal provider. Earlier in the book we reported that 60 percent of all mothers do not know what they are cooking for dinner at 4 PM. At this time, many moms are shuttling their children from activity to activity in their vehicles with the radio playing loudly. This is the perfect time for a meal planner to suggest its quick-and-easy dinner solution to this tired, busy mom. This is what we call being in the right place at the right time with the right solution. Radio is economical as well. In some markets, a 60-second spot can cost as little as $25. The second type of marketing tool available in radio is custom programming. This was the niche that Maria filled when she created Mom Talk Radio for a client. Through purchasing brokered time, she was able to develop a program completely focused on mom issues from health to finances to parenting. The strategy works well because it connects the sponsor with moms by providing them with useful information in a convenient format.

PARTNERSHIPS

Partnerships can be very valuable tools in connecting with moms. The right partnership between two companies can take each participant into a new venue and allow the consumer to interact with the brand in a new arena. For instance, the past year's partnership between Oreos and Universal Studios put *The Grinch* video on the cookie aisle of major retailers. Because the two products were bundled, moms were able to interact with both brands in a new way.

The right partnership can also bring a brand to life for the consumer. An example is the recent partnership between Holiday Inn Family Suites and Nickelodeon. Both brands deliver family fun in two different venues: one as a vacation destination and one through television programming. In 2005, they will open the Nickelodeon Family Suites by Holiday Inn in Orlando, Florida. The family destination will incorporate Nickelodeon personalities into a multi-million-dollar pool area, themed rooms, and entertainment center. For moms and their families, this will bring to life the programming they enjoy at home and deliver the brand message to them at a time spent outside their living rooms. This strategy appeals to both Gen X and Gen Y moms who are used to experiencing brand messaging in various areas of their lives, whether through music or when shopping in a mall.

Marketing partnerships also make sense in the Mom Market because they link solutions with lifestyle traits. To determine the right partnership for your brand or product, find a universal mom challenge, similar to an urban legend, a situation that all moms can relate to. For example, a problem faced by moms when traveling with their children is how to pack snacks without taking along the entire bag of chips, dried fruit, or cookies, and leaving some to grow stale. One solution is to use Ziploc bags. In one of the best marketing partnerships we've seen in a long time, Ziploc bags ran a sweepstakes giving away a family vacation; its copy offered this advice: When you leave, keep your food fresh by using Ziploc bags. What this idea did was to marry a basic everyday challenge of a mother with an easy answer. Most important, it told the mom that Ziploc *got* it. It made the consumer feel like Ziploc had spied into her kitchen. There's a lot more opportunities for similar types of question-and-answer marketing. What mom doesn't pack a roll of paper towels in the van when it's time for a summer road trip? A similar promotion could involve a drive destination or hotel change and a paper towel brand. And what if mothers all over the country knew that the secret to removing playground sand off a child's feet was to sprinkle baby powder on and brush with your hand. Magically, the sand is removed. We suspect that a greater number of moms would carry Johnson & Johnson Baby Powder to the park. Tie in the message with a day-at-the-park giveaway that might include bikes, picnic supplies, and a tote that included baby powder to remove the sand.

As the emerging Generation Ys who tend to be more philanthropic become moms, partnerships with community groups will be effective. For example, there's more than one way to slice an apple and the Produce Marketing Association (PMA) looks at marketing in the same creative way. To promote its 5 A Day campaign, the PMA encourages its members to hold free health screenings and offer nutrients advice on diets and eating habits. This is a creative way to communicate the health benefits of their products while providing a service to the community. Corporations are always looking for participants at their company-sponsored health days, while community health expos are looking for services to provide to their attendees. Often the cost is minimal or, in many instances, may even be free. The cost merely covers the expense of having someone in the booth throughout the event and giving away some type of premium. Many times you can easily find volunteers among your employees who for a day off during the week would gladly work a Saturday at a festival or fair. The direct interaction with consumers is often a positive experience for employees and provides valuable feedback about the public's perception of your product.

SPECIAL EVENTS

We recently asked mothers about the effectiveness of special events in marketing products and services to them. Surprisingly, only 30 percent said that special events were good ways to market to mothers. The answer didn't seem to mesh with all the crowded convention center shows, expos, and fairs we've attended. There seemed to be lots of moms with strollers cruising the aisles of booths, picking up samples of products along the way. So we began asking vendors at these events what kind of responses they received from prospective customers. Interestingly, those who invested in booth space told us that big shows didn't really pay off for them. They agreed that lots of moms attended, but for some reason they weren't spending a lot of time learning about products or services. After numerous interviews and additional work with moms, we found that special events are indeed successful in marketing to moms, but that the types of special events moms want to attend are different from the ones where vendors were buying booth space. Although moms are attending these big events, their purpose in attending was not to make buying decisions but rather to entertain their children. Event planners had included kids' activities in their shows' agendas in a way to keep moms there for a long time, and as the number of show attendees increased, so did the scale of the children's entertainment. "Word of mom" went to work and spread the news that these events were perfect for tiring out the kids for nap time. In other words, the purpose of the events in the eyes of the events organizers was quite different than the way moms viewed it. Regardless of the disconnect between events managers and moms, today's moms enjoy the intimacy of peer groups, book clubs, and bible studies, and thus value special events of another size. They want to attend smaller events that focus on singular topics where they can trade ideas with other moms who share their interests. A good example of the value today's moms place on smaller special-interest events can be seen in the popularity of the Mommy and Me programs. The company that offers programming for mom groups across the United States now has more than 80,000 registered groups according to their CEO, June Pemberton. It's an organic growth of mothers coming together to create small events, sometimes weekly, for other mothers in their communities. By examining the clubs and groups that moms are forming, whether Mommy and Me or MOM clubs, marketers can see that the ages of the mothers may vary, but the ages of the children fit within developmental age groups. The groups are organic in nature based on the kids' activities and the lifestyle traits of the mothers.

Marketers today need to change their thinking about special events. In addition to using smaller venues, marketers should produce events that include educationally focused programs that allow mothers to grow in some way. Hospitals have capitalized on the new behavior of mothers by offering classes that address everything from introducing babies to music to daddy diapering. If you doubt their popularity, take a ride over to your local parenting center to see rooms full of mommies sitting in circles learning the latest in mommy skills.

A few retailers have also benefited by bringing moms together to learn. The most documented is Lowe's, the home-improvement giant. By offering do-it-yourself lessons, it grew its sales by capturing the hearts of females it empowered with the knowledge of how to use its products. The awareness of classes such as "How to Sponge-Paint Your Nursery" spread with the speed of viral marketing. Suddenly, Lowe's had moms learning to do everything from laying tile to installing ceiling fans to building tree forts with their children. These small events produced big sales for Lowe's.

Wal-Mart recently partnered with Todobebe.com, the leading online destination for Spanish-speaking mothers. Together they are producing small one-day events focused on the Latino mother, which are held in the parking lot of select Wal-Mart stores. The brainchild of Gillian Sandler, the company's CEO, this is a good example of targeting a specific segment of mothers who share a lifestyle and a life stage. Through their partnership with Todobebe.com, the big-box retailer is able to deliver the special event experience to thousands of moms online as well as to those who attend in person.

CAUSE-RELATED MARKETING

One type of event that has remained effective in marketing to moms is the event that is linked to a particular cause. Special events such as walk-a-thons, runs, bike-a-thons, and collections that benefit nonprofit organizations always appeal to mothers, especially if they see a direct benefit for their children. We see continued growth in these events as the philanthropic Gen Y women become mothers. The appeal of cause-related events is not limited to young mothers; boomer and Gen X moms are being drawn to events such as marathons and endurance rides that present them with opportunities for growth. Today, some marathons boast a field of more than 30,000 runners, many of whom are females. The performance of thirtysomething athletes such as Deena Kastor, 31, who won the bronze medal for the United States in the women's marathon at the 2004 Olympics in Athens, Greece, has boosted the popularity of such extreme sports with older women.

Companies who cross the line from marketing to community relations will see a payoff in sales. Moms tell us that they are more likely to purchase products from companies who support the community in which they are raising their children. The most recognized programs by mothers are Newman's Own Salad Dressings, Ben & Jerry's Ice Cream, and Avon's Pink Ribbon programs. Gen Ys who have a tendency to be philanthropic in nature have popularized two brands of jeans because of their cause tie-in, Serve the People and Citizens of Humanity.

ENTERTAINING MOMS

Time and time again we hear from moms that when it comes to marketing, companies forget that moms like to laugh and have fun. The concept seems adverse to the job that moms have in creating happy times for their families, but this is what they tell us.

Our research showed that nearly 90 percent of mothers across the board believe that a sense of humor is a trait of a great mom. She wants to be entertained and, in turn, she looks

Eighty-five percent of mothers say a sense of humor is an important trait for their children to develop.

Ninety-five percent of moms try to laugh with their families on a regular basis.

for companies and brands that can laugh with her.

Entertainment is one way that companies can connect with moms and their children in a lighthearted experiential manner. It's just another way to allow moms to experience your brand rather than reading about its benefits.

Theme parks have been allowing families to live their brands through entertainment for many years. Disney, of course, is the master of such marketing and because there are enough of its case studies to fill a library, we choose to talk about a few others. Hershey Park is an example of another company that not only created an entertainment park around its brand but also turned its factory into an educational experience for families. It gives moms the option of spending a day on rides or riding through a class on the production of chocolate. One way or the other, the entire family is experiencing the brand through every one of their five senses, from smelling the irresistible aroma of candy kisses to the feel of cocoa beans. And what you can't take with you, the company will ship home so it's waiting for you long after the sensations of the day have faded.

A different type of entertainment experience can be found in Atlanta, Georgia, at The World of Coca-Cola. Similar to Hershey, the beverage giant has created a destination that allows families to interact with its brand besides just drinking it.

Not every company is large enough to build a theme park or a destination around its product. However, every retail brand has the opportunity to win the hearts of moms by creating a rewarding experience of another kind every time moms walk through the doors.

RETAIL EXPERIENCE

Companies spend millions of dollars each year attempting to get moms to walk through their doors. Many are very successful, but, unfortunately, they fail to win the mother as a customer because she has indeed walked through their doors. The retail experience of a mom cannot be ignored as part of your overall marketing strategy.

Potty Time

"Mommy, I have to use the potty" are often the first words a mother will hear on entering your store. No, it's not your greeter. It's the biological alarm that seems to sound in children when they enter a new environment. Their amusement with discovering new bathrooms translates into every mother's drudgery. We assure you that first impressions do matter in this area. The first stop we always make when evaluating a retail location is the bathroom, mainly because it is often your mom customer's first stop as well. Your bathroom should be clean, bright, and free from any overwhelming artificial perfume smells. Most operation executives are wise enough to put a changing table in their restrooms, but it's not enough to stop there. Toddler chairs or hooks to hang diaper bags on tell a mom you care about her business. Recently, we disclosed to a client that was determined to attract moms that its bathrooms were bare any tampon machines. This small detail had been overlooked by a totally male facilities team but it would certainly trigger a fast departure by female customers.

Unfortunately, we do not have the pages to detail every aspect of the optimum mom shopping experience but a few features are important. Consider aisle size and physical layout. Can her stroller fit down your aisle easily? Mothers who cannot walk down your aisles can't buy your merchandise. Remember that the safety of her children is her most important concern. We visited one store location that positioned a large gumball machine between the outside and inside automatic doors more than ten feet from the register lines. Every time a child ran to the gumball machine, the outside automatic doors exposed him or her to the busy parking lot and to an uninhibited escape from his or her mother. This was an accident waiting to happen, and more often than not, moms ran out of the register line to chase their children. We watched as many frustrated moms walked right out the doors without making their purchases. Keeping her children safe is just one way of making the shopping experience enjoyable. We love the idea of stork or stroller parking, because it shows moms pulling into your parking lot that you understand the challenge of moving children from a parking lot to the sidewalk. If your Realtor will permit such signage, it's a great way to win the hearts of moms.

Merchandising

It's worthwhile to talk briefly about merchandising as part of the mom shopping experience. Moms are constantly looking for solutions, and this is true in the aisles of your store as well. Although they may enjoy the hunt for a bargain, they do not appreciate hunting for a product with cranky children in tow. Moms apply intuition to their shopping experience so it's important that your merchandising reflects the intuitive nature of a mom. Something as simple as offering batteries next to a toy that requires two AAAs can go a long way to making the experience positive for her. To increase a mom's shopping cart share, it's imperative to understand the lifestyle elements that prompt her to buy in your store. For instance, are moms coming to purchase quick and easy birthday gifts for her child's overscheduled social calendar? If so, why not offer gift cards and wrap near such products?

Bundling products has become a popular merchandising method particularly when targeting moms. It makes it easy and convenient for mothers to grab and go with your product.

PRODUCT AND PACKAGING

Some might wonder how a discussion on product and packaging finds itself in a chapter on words in motion. We assure you it was not by accident. The marketing messages you develop for your company will travel in many different ways. One way is in the packaging of your product. Before you toss this responsibility to another department, we'd like you to consider how it impacts moms and how it can be integrated within your marketing play beyond the obvious words on the box. Let's talk first about the form of your product. All through this book, we've reminded you that moms want to know that "you get them." One way to do this is to understand how they are using your product and to make modifications that reinforce or welcome that behavior. After all, your best customer is one who is already buying your product so why not encourage her to buy more by adapting it to her needs. Recall our example of juice boxes and mothers who use them as ice packs. This is only one product that takes on a new shape and size in the eyes of mothers. Consider peanut butter. Who would have ever imagined that our children—and we—would suck peanut butter out of a plastic tube? For years, moms have been either smacking the fingers of little hands from dipping into the jar or serving eager snackers scoops of Peter Pan on spoons. By understanding consumer behavior, this brand was able to develop an entirely new product line from an old staple. Moms love it because it offers a solution to a long-standing challenge—how to package individual servings of peanut butter for lunch boxes and snack bags.

Another great example is cereal bars. Recognizing the importance of breakfast and the challenge of time in the morning, moms were eager for new breakfast options. For years, mothers have been filling snack bags with cereal and allowing their children to "go milkless." Product development teams were smart enough to act on this behavior and produce a solution to their challenge. The result of their innovation was the growth of a new food bar category that boasts sales of $2.9 million.[3] Today, food in the form of to-go bars is not only finding its way into school car pools but also into lunch boxes and onto athletic fields.

We call this creative way of thinking "shifting the shape." Look at your product—size, shape, and style—and see if it can be altered in a way that fills a new need or taps an old practice. The result may not only gain you sales in the Mom Market, but it may earn you a "They get me" from your best customers.

The obvious marketing opportunities in packaging lie in the words on your box or hangtags. This written message will communicate with your customer every time he or she touches your product. Think of it with the same value as you would shelf space in a major retailer. In fact, it may be worth even more because it presents a more intimate relationship between you and the end user. Think about how long some boxes inhabit prime real estate in a mom's cabinet or refrigerator. Arm & Hammer Baking Soda comes to mind. This product stays in the kitchen so long that the company has to remind customers to throw it out! Wouldn't that be a good problem to have? Every time a mom opens her freezer there's the yellow billboard reinforcing its promise to keep her food tasting fresh and to eliminate smells. The same can be said for items such as Bisquick, Worchester Sauce, and vanilla. All are staples that a mom keeps on hand but may use infrequently. The opportunity for these companies is to educate moms on new ways to utilize their companies' products, increasing consumption and repurchasing at the same time. This can be accomplished not only through words on your packaging but by directing moms to your Web site or customer-service lines. Discovery is part of the appeal to moms, so you may want to lead them toward points of discovery such as new recipes or craft ideas. The space, of course, can be used to promote special events, partnerships, and promotions.

We encourage clients to look at all the available white space on their packages and, as already suggested a number of times, determine how the customers are using their packages. We recognize that in many cases the package is opened and then tossed in the garbage, but this is not always the case. The best example of this is a box of checks. Working with Clarke American, the leading supplier of printed checks, we learned that a large number of women retain the boxes in which they receive their checks. They place a high value on these boxes and thus they choose to keep them in a safe place. Interestingly, this often includes the top drawer of a woman's bureau or desk. Many women even told us that they keep their boxes of checks in their underwear drawers next to their Victoria Secrets. This is great brand association for Clarke American! By looking at the placement of the product's package and the behavior of the consumer, we realized that these women were looking at the tops of their check boxes every time they opened their drawers. Ironically, the top of the box rarely carries any marketing messages. This is the perfect spot to list other bank services to remind the patron to come back for more or to thank her for her business. In addition, there is an opportunity to print messages on the underside of the box lid, which a woman flips open, exposing the now white space every time she retrieves a new box of checks.

WORD OF MOUTH

Nothing moves words faster through the Mom Market than moms. We've mentioned the importance of word-of-mouth marketing throughout this book and how powerful it can be when it comes to mom. Like a wildfire, it can spread rapidly and bring you thousands if not millions of new customers. What we haven't examined, however, is what exactly acts as the first spark to ignite this change of events. When moms start talking about a product, they tell peer after peer about it. It's a phenomenon that Jackie Huba, coauthor of *Creating Customer Evangelists: How*

Loyal Customers Become a Volunteer Sales Force, terms *customer evangelism.* "Moms are often searching for products and services that solve problems. If a product solves a big problem, it may literally change a mom's life. That can translate into evangelism among other moms, even those who have yet to publicly voice their problem. For marketers, this requires a close understanding of the word on the street," describes Huba.

We never like to focus on the negative but sometimes there are lessons to be learned by someone else's marketing challenges. If you ever doubted the effectiveness of word-of-mouth marketing in the Mom Market, recall what happened to Oreos recently. On the wings of media attention regarding child obesity, message board postings, and chat-room discussions, the word spread quickly that one of America's favorite cookies was one of the most fattening. Almost overnight, the years of the memorable appeal of dunking an Oreo in milk was erased. It took quick action and crisis public relations on the part of Nabisco to bring the wildfire under control.

In contrast, mom's enthusiasm for Pinxav Diaper Rash Ointment has kept this small brand of diaper rash defense alive in the marketplace since 1927. You won't find Pinxav in full-page ads in the parenting publications, but you will find mom testimonials saturating baby and mom Web sites all over the Internet. The buzz in nurseries across the United States has earned the trust of moms and translated into sales for Pinxav.

Delivering on brand promises and providing great customer service are two ways to cultivate a sales force for your company around the playground, in pediatricians' waiting rooms, and on the mat at Gymboree. Moms who have a good experience will share it with other moms. Have you wondered why word of mouth is so effective in the Mom Market? Why word spreads so quickly? In most cases moms spread information because of their inherent need to nurture. By helping another mom find a product or solution, she feels she is helping her peer save the time otherwise spent researching the product. In addition, an answer to another mom's problem is a way for her to demonstrate her own knowledge and experience as a mom. It's a way to show that's she's weathered the storm of diapers and come out with some type of know-how that puts value on her own experience. You'll also find that in the world of moms, certain mothers seem to be influencers within their peer groups; these moms are Mavens. These are the moms who always have the answers and/or have earned the respect of other moms for one reason or another. Normally, her position in the hierarchy of peers was earned because of the experiences that reach beyond those of the rest of the group. These experiences may include raising twins or exceptionally large families.

A mom's status within a peer group can also be based on the behavior of her children. Moms of well-behaved, honor students as well as mothers of special-needs children rank high among other moms. There are, of course, those moms who always have an opinion on everything, but we do not define them as influencers. Their words often fall on deaf ears because they are heard so often that they lose credibility. We must warn you, however, that you do not want to get these women on your bad side. They will talk about a negative experience with every person they encounter, male or female. This is the one time when others do perk up their ears to her message and one bad experience can erase ten good ones.

It's important for marketers to learn who the Mavens are in their target markets. You may find that moms of toddlers are telling your story to moms of newborns or that older moms within a school send peers to your Web site. We know this task might seem like finding a needle in a haystack in a market of 73 million moms, but we assure you it's much easier. Next Saturday, find a playing field in your city and go sit in the stands with the moms for a few hours. It won't take long for you to identify the Maven, who holds the keys to knowledge. After a few Saturdays, you'll soon be able to see a trend in her age, socioeconomic position, and the ages of her children. We believe that in today's Mom Market where you find boomer moms interacting with Gen X and Gen Y mothers with children of the same age, the Boomer rises as an influencer. In most cases, she'll earn the respect of younger moms by virtue of the expanded experiences her life span has offered her. In this case, it's the collection of knowledge she can share rather than just the answer she provides to other mothers.

Keep in mind also our earlier discussion about the effectiveness of peer spokespeople as part of your public relations campaigns. The influencers you identify can make excellent spokespersons on a local or regional level. Sometimes by following the chain of information, you can identify the moms who have established themselves as connectors on a national level. They aren't necessarily the Katie Couric or Kelly Ripa moms of the world, but they might be moms who have virtual networks via the Internet or articles they have authored. Some of these mom peer leaders may have audiences of one or two million moms. These are the mothers you want talking about your product.

So how do you create the buzz that turns mothers into evangelists for your brand? Huba says it's by asking two important questions: "Marketers can understand what people are saying by asking, 'Would you recommend our product?' and 'What exactly would you say about it?'" She adds that if the answer to the first question is no, it's important to find out why.

One way to discover what customers are saying about you is to listen. We, of course, endorse good research that can allow you to hear from customers and prospective customers, but here we offer additional opportunities for dialogue. Some of the best feedback can be obtained from moms you probably already have contact with in the form of suggestion e-mails and complaint cards. Every one of these seemingly negative opinions can be turned into a positive for you and your brand. If moms are telling you that they want your product container to be larger in size, than they are telling others that they can never keep enough on hand. You're hearing that it's an inconvenience for her to constantly replenish her stock. We suggest you find a box of processed complaint cards and read through them wearing a new pair of glasses, looking for trends and commonalities. You must read beyond the words on the page and imagine what preceded or followed the suggestions. Imagine moms sitting in the bleachers next Saturday using the words on the cards and ask yourself, What would the rest of the conversation sound like?

Another way to find out what moms are saying is to ask them to contact you. Most companies list an 800 customer-service number on their packaging or marketing materials; few, however, fully utilize its potential. If a customer, especially a busy mom, cares enough to call you, she's likely to be willing to share her opinions and ideas with you. So instead of allowing only customer-service representatives to encounter this wealth of customer knowledge, give your marketing team access to these calls as well.

Nestlé recently tested this idea with Turtles candy. Internally, the company considered package changes for the caramel-and-nut sweet and, in fact, thought about eliminating the Mr. Turtle character from the box. Although it conducted focus groups around these ideas, ultimately it was the opinions of callers that swayed its decision. Mr. Turtle remains on the box today and Nestlé has discovered a new source for customer insights.

Remember to give moms more than one way to communicate with you. Generation Y moms in particular expect to be able to e-mail, Instant Message, or even text message you with ideas, suggestions, and comments.

Once you discover what the word on the street is about your product or service, you can apply the knowledge to the message insights and marketing initiatives we've examined thus far.

CUSTOMER SERVICE

As a marketer you most likely will focus your energy on creating a buzz in the marketplace through creative campaigns or any one of the numerous marketing initiatives available to you in the Mom Market. Regardless of the strategy you choose to execute, the one that should not be overlooked is customer service. Unfortunately, this responsibility normally lies within the operations division of most companies and is left untouched by marketers. We cannot stress enough just how important good customer service is in getting moms to talk about your brand.

We would even go as far as to say that once all product promises are met, it's the service after the sale that will serve as the point of differentiation. As we've already discussed, some mothers will pay more for good customer service. It means that much to them. Good customer service is achieved by exceeding the customer's expectations. Notice we didn't say "meeting their expectations." This is because moms in general expect some level of service and poor delivery has taught them to expect less than what they should receive. So by meeting their expectations, you are actually not impressing them enough to get them talking. You want to "wow" them in some way that excites them. Moms thrive on passion—for their children and for their families— and they identify this in others as well. If you demonstrate a passion for delivering the best possible customer service, then you'll win their hearts. The good news for marketers is that it doesn't take much to go above and beyond for mothers. Normally. it's as easy as adding one or two new procedures or policies to operations already in place. For instance, moms are master schedulers. Their job as keeper of the household calendar requires them to be. Moms take great pride in and experience a sense of accomplishment getting their kids from Boy Scouts to basketball on time. So when it comes to home-delivery services, they expect others to respect their time restraints. You may think your company is doing well in regards to customer service because you have a 90 percent on-time delivery rate. You tell a mom that you'll be there at 10 AM with the new freezer she bought on Sunday and you are there at 10 AM. But what if you exceeded her expectations? What could that do for your business?

City Furniture, a leading furniture retailer in the Southeast, not only gives its customers a time for delivery, but it arms its drivers with cell phones to call customers when they are en route. If they intend to be early, they call to ask if it's convenient to arrive sooner than expected. The procedure not only calls attention to the early delivery time but says to a mom, "We respect your time and do not assume we can drop in whenever it's convenient for us." We're not sure Keith Koenig, founder of City Furniture, considered this point but it also appeals to a woman's sense of security. No mother wants to be caught in the shower by a delivery man knocking at the front door. It's a courtesy that goes a long way to motivating mothers to share their customer experience. It must work because we wouldn't be writing about it if one of us had not experienced it firsthand.

Another easy-to-execute customer-service feature that goes a long way with moms is referring to them by name. Some retailers such as grocers have moved in this direction. The strategy works because moms, although women with children, like to maintain their own identities. In fact, many sometimes complain that their names are lost in their roles as Junior's mom or Sam's wife. By addressing her by her name, your customer-service representatives or cashiers are saying they care not only about her as a person but recognize her as a customer. It also links her to a time when retailers maintained an intimate relationship with their customers. Most companies execute this practice by having frontline personnel learn customer names from credit cards or other identification at the time of transaction.

Finally, don't forget to say "thank you." It's one of the first lessons in manners that a mother teaches her child. If she didn't value it so much, she wouldn't put it so high on the list of lessons she passes along to her child. It's one marketing tip you can credit your own mother for providing you.

Once you've put down this book and you've written your marketing plan, take a minute—maybe more—to examine the operations that support your messaging. See if there are ways for you to go above and beyond your customers' expectations. Moms show their appreciation by telling other mothers, putting your marketing messages into motion. Finding the right delivery channel to put your brand messages into motion to increase sales or retail traffic can mean the difference between success and lackluster results. The words you take so much care into formulating will be useless unless applied to the right marketing initiative—whether it's in television, radio, special events, or unique retail experiences. Remember the goal of setting your brand promises into motion is to generate a buzz that produces a wave of word of mouth in the Mom Market. Once you get the right moms talking about your product or service, they will carry your message beyond the pages of your advertising or Web site. These mom influencers will become your Mom Mavens and evangelists trumpeting your message to moms along the way to school, in the office, and at home. Your marketing initiatives must be backed by superior customer service because moms expect you to understand their need for speed, convenience, and dependability. In return for your efforts, moms will deliver the actions you desire at the cash register.

12

MOMS ONLINE
AND UNPLUGGED

For generations, moms have longed for an extra hour in their day or for a personal assistant to help juggle the demands of being a mother. These prayers seem to be answered with the birth of the Internet and the subsequent advances in wireless technology. Fortunately for marketers, the stampede of moms toward the Internet also opened hundreds if not thousands of new points of connection with them. Although Gen X and Gen Y had the advantage of being raised with technology, it hasn't taken long for Baby Boomers to see the value of the Internet as a partner in parenting. Moms of all generations now use the technology to help them. Literally thousands of applications for the Internet help mothers juggle the challenges of being a household CEO, business owner, wife, chauffeur, and parent. Regardless of the roles moms play daily in their families, the Internet is an important tool.

Mothers have found ways to utilize the Internet to simplify their lives. If they face a challenge or need product information or validation, they go to the Internet. If she is a pregnant mother looking for a name for her baby, she can search the baby name database at http://www.storkavenue.com, or chat with other home-based working mothers at http://www.hbwm.com, or plan her child's school fundraiser at http://www.chuckecheese .com, or plan for her baby at http://www.babiesonline.com.

Today's mothers are online in record numbers and marketers can expect the numbers to grow as Generation Y women begin having children. This latter cohort was born into technology and they are quite confident in their abilities to utilize it in their role as mothers. The numbers speak to the incredible opportunities that exist to connect with moms online.

THE NUMBERS

A study released by Pew Internet and American Life Project following the 2001 holiday season indicates that more women than ever shop on the Internet. The survey showed that of the 29 million American shoppers who bought gifts online during the 2001 holiday season, 58 percent were women.[1] More than 16 million eager women are ready to visit your site, and the best part is that with the right Web site, you can serve them 24 hours a day, 7 days a week.[2]

A recent Gallup poll reported that in the United States there are an estimated 21.2 million Web-surfing mothers, followed by Great Britain with 2.2 million, and 1.5 million in France. Moms are not only surfing the Web and spending money, they also are spending more time on the Internet than they are watching television. In research conducted in conjunction with *Marketing to Moms* (Prima, 2002), 88 percent of moms said they rely on the Web for parental guidance, advice, and ideas for raising their children. Eighty-six percent said they made an online purchase, while 85 percent said they clicked on an online ad, and 95 percent said they are online at least once a day.

SEEKERS NOT BROWSERS

Moms are seekers not browsers when they go online. Although this behavior has largely been dictated by their busy schedules, the online experience of younger moms will continue this trend. Gen X and Gen Y moms know how to navigate quickly through Web sites, search engines, and databases of information. They are proud of their knowledge and don't spend a lot of time dealing with online destinations that don't provide them with what they seek.

We've conducted numerous research projects throughout the years on how moms are using the Internet and each one has produced the same results. Moms are going online for information. In fact, in a study with Lucid Marketing, a leading provider of e-mail communication, more than half of the mothers surveyed would want access to e-mail if they were stranded on a desert island.

In another recent poll, we asked moms where they go for information about their children's development. Forty-five percent said the Internet, which scored five points higher than their pediatricians did. We also asked what specifically they wanted when they went online. Overwhelmingly, they said solutions to challenges they had as moms. Their needs can include anything from a medical explanation to craft ideas. We asked this same group of mothers what were the top four reasons they visited or revisited a Web site. Their answers, in order of popularity, were: expert advice, quick and easy tips, news on child-related issues, and special values.

To capture large numbers of moms online, it's important to create a Web site that will provide moms with the information they are seeking in a format that will keep them coming back. Let's get started.

WEB SITES

The key to creating a Web site that successfully attracts and retains moms is to provide the valuable information they need in an easy-to-find format. For this reason, your home page is an important starting point. Consider this your book cover. Within 30 seconds, a mom will decide by the look of your cover whether it's worth reading. In the case of your Web site, your home page will instantly tell her if she wants to stay. Just a quick note about that first 30 seconds—make sure that your Web site loads quickly. If you use some type of Flash technology that delays a mom when she's trying to reach your home page, she'll likely leave before she ever gets inside. Additionally, many younger technology-savvy moms don't want to watch the same introduction every time they visit your site. Once they've seen it, they don't need to see it again. By incorporating flashy introduction pages, you've backed yourself into a corner that either bores your technology-savvy customers or requires you to make expensive changes to your Web site regularly. We suggest creating a clean home page that contains one or two easily dynamic features or interactive tools that will appeal to a younger multimedia generation of mothers. Depending on the focus of your product or brand, you might consider a one-question, online poll somewhere on the front page. Moms love to see what other moms are thinking and will often answer an online survey to see how their replies stack up against the answers of other mothers. This feature also appeals to their desire for immediate gratification and establishes you as a provider of up-to-date information. If you are an astute marketer, you will use your online poll to obtain quick and easy information on your customers. It can become a cost-effective means to maintaining a pulse on your moms.

WEB SITE GPS

Another important element of your home page is your navigation. It's the first impression a mom gets telling her whether your site is easy to use. Remember, she always wants to save time, so if it looks like it will take her more time to navigate your site than it will to search for another source, she's gone. Navigation should be intuitive to the lifestyle of a mother. For instance, if she visits your site for career information, link the content with other topics that relate to channels that provide her with daycare information, easy meal-planning ideas, and work and family balance articles. As a smart marketer, you are assuming that a mom reading career information is either a working mother or one that is contemplating returning to work after having a baby. By showing your knowledge of her lifestyle, you demonstrate to her that as a working mom her challenges lie in caring for her children, feeding them after a long day at the office, and trying to manage her dual role as mother and career woman. This approach puts all she needs at her fingertips and, more important, keeps her on your Web site. As a marketer, you have created a meaningful dialogue with this mother and established your brand as a resource. She'll be back because she knows you understand her.

Because a mom is most likely coming to your site for content, carefully consider how you arrange it for her. We suggest organizing it either by lifestyle groups or by the ages of her children. The latter works well for content relating to the development of her children or activities that she can share with them. Thus, a mother of a teenager doesn't have to sort through numerous articles on potty training when all she wants is help managing homework. If its food products you sell, sort them by the uses a mom might have for them. For instance, you might sort marshmallows into categories such as Craft Projects, Fun Foods, Dessert Ideas, or Food Toppings. What you are telling your mom is that you understand she uses your product in a variety of ways and you want to help her save time by making it easy to find what she needs. You *get* her!

Unfortunately, we don't have the pages to dive deeply into all the visual and graphic elements of a successful Web site. We do, however, feel it is important to mention briefly two elements that deserve your attention. First is color. Do not assume that because you are designing a site for women that it should be pink. In fact, don't use pink. Moms today, regardless of generation, are not inclined to be more attracted to this hue. It's been overused, and to many, it represents an outdated representation of motherhood. In fact, we suggest staying away from the traditional pastel blues, yellows, and pinks unless it is absolutely necessary for branding purposes. Select more natural colors and incorporate a hip and edgy tone to appeal to younger moms. The second point we want to touch on briefly is graphics. Just as with your print materials, make certain that the pictures you select reflect your audience. Recently, we evaluated the Web site of a client who was trying to attract moms to purchase online. The site provided terrific content and allowed friendly navigation, but when we clicked to its product page, we didn't find one picture of a woman. In fact, it showed a twenty-something male peddling appliances. There was no relevance to the audience at all and the visitors certainly could not picture themselves with the merchandise. Remember that moms appreciate reality and for them it's about kids, family, and moms like themselves.

Becky Chao, Marketing Manager for Nestlé Infant Nutrition, says the success of a mom Web site is based on the relevance of its content and tools to her lifestyle as a mother. "In addition to being extremely easy to navigate, a Web site needs to provide content and tools that help to simplify, support, and celebrate her experience as a new mom. The best way to achieve this is to base the development on a thorough understanding of key 'mom insights,'" Chao says.

Key Elements to a Successful Mom Web Site

• Easy navigation

• About Us section

• Contact Information on top of home page

• Privacy policy

• Site search

• Latest news

• Electronic newsletter registration

• Top ten lists

• Interactive tools

• Archived articles

• Online polls

Hundreds of companies are operating great Web sites for moms. Based on the number of active URLs, there are millions. We chose to examine just a few as a way to illustrate what makes a good destination for mothers.

First, let's visit Nestlé's Web site, http://www.verybestbaby .com. The success of this Web site that moms find today did not come without trials. Nestlé began its Web site adventures as a product information site and ultimately it evolved into an information destination that provides the company with indirect consumer sales and branding opportunities. Once Nestlé discovered that content was the best strategy for connecting its brands to mothers, the company found many ways to integrate this strategy into its brand product Web sites. Nestlé's Web strategy now focuses on creating sites that help and inform consumers. Each of its sites carries the ubiquitous "very best" slogan in the URL and draws on the common functionality and customer language. Moms who visit http://www.verybestbaby.com can find helpful information about recovering after birth, what it means to be a mother, health advice, a weight tracker, and even breast-feeding tips. It may seem unlikely to get all this from a company who wants to sell moms GOOD START® formula for their babies, but it works. The strategy gives Nestlé the most valuable opportunity in marketing—the chance to develop an interactive and loyal relationship with its customers. This strategy allows the company to develop credibility and trust, an emotional tie difficult to create through a stagnant advertisement.

In addition to http://www.verybestbaby.com, Nestlé provides resource content through http://www.verybestmeals.com, http://www.verybestkids.com, http://www.verybestbaking.com, and http://www.verybestpet.com.

Another site that we think has done a good job in understanding moms is Fisher-Price, http://www.fisherprice.com. What's unique about this Web site is that it demonstrates through its content that the company understands what moms are doing with its products. Originally, the site contained predominantly product information and activities that moms could play with their children. It contained printable coloring sheets for children, online games, and stories. It also provided moms with suggested birthday present ideas that, in turn, sold its products. Today, however, it's a mecca of great content and tools for moms. Not only can a mom now find the perfect birthday gift, she can find information on throwing a great birthday bash for her child; instead of just toy descriptions, she can find articles on how to enhance the learning experience while playing with a particular toy. Moms can send electronic cards to other moms to learn about children with special needs or to get expert parenting advice. What Fisher-Price did was to integrate its brand and products into the lifestyle of its mom audience through content and tools that provided valuable information and quick solutions. This is an extremely well-executed Web site.

You don't have to be a big-name brand to create a good online destination for moms. Thousands of smaller sites exist, many of which are run by passionate mothers, that attract large numbers of mothers. Not only do these smaller sites serve as good examples of online successes, but they also should not be ignored when identifying places to advertise online. We suggest visiting some of our favorites: http://www.amazingmoms.com, http://www.babiesonline.com, http://www.bellaonline.com, http://www.sheknows.com, and, of course, our own http://www.bluesuitmom.com.

E-COMMERCE

Moms are doing more than just searching for information online. They are purchasing products as well. A study commissioned by the Walt Disney Group's Disney Online, conducted by C&R Research, reports that there are 31 million moms online.[3]

The number is growing every day as Internet-savvy Gen Xers and Gen Ys begin to purchase products for their new babies and growing families. More importantly to the topic of e-commerce, women are spending more online than men are. According to a report by Jupiter Media Metrix on the 2001 holiday spending, women represented 53 percent of the $11.9 billion spent online. The most popular categories for female purchases included CDs, books, health and beauty aids, toys, and apparel for both herself and her children.

When building an e-commerce site for mothers, you must remember that they are very busy people. They like to find solutions to simplify their lives, save time, and help them work more efficiently. They appreciate doing business with companies who relate to their needs. Additionally, when it comes to online purchases, they want to have a heightened level of trust in doing business with you. The latter is the most important issue to address if you want to capture a mother's online sale. Their concerns relate to personal privacy, lack of Internet regulation, stolen credit card numbers, and other transactions. In a 2000 survey by Cyber Dialogue, 40 percent said they are concerned about the security of the information they give on sites.[4]

The lack of trust in your security measures can translate to the loss of big bucks. The same study pointed out that women who felt safe buying online spent an average of $830 compared to $459 spent by doubting females.[5] Your first priority in designing your e-commerce site should be to establish trust in your potential customers. You can tell moms it's safe to do business with you by clearly displaying your privacy policy on the home page of your site. You also want to let them know how to contact you in the case of a problem.

Once you've established trust, you want to make the buying experience as seamless as possible. Bob Hunter, CEO of Stork-Avenue, the largest printable birth announcement company in the United States, believes intuition is the most important element to a good buying experience for his expectant and new mothers.

"An e-commerce Web site should be an intelligent cash register. It should be intuitive to the customers needs and recognize what the customer wants while making it easy for them to buy the product," explains Hunter, whose online sales now account for more than 40 percent of his annual sales. "If you ask the right questions, you can lead the consumer to the sale. They will make an informed decision and feel good about their purchases."

Hunter goes the extra steps to ensure repeat business. Each order is followed by a confirmation e-mail, a shipping message, and a thank-you note. These elements not only are part of the checkout process, but they represent another key component to executing a successful e-commerce strategy: customer service.

The Holiday Inn Family Suites™ site, at http://www.hifamilysuites.com, was designed to be not only a booking engine for hotel stays, but, by realizing the importance of allowing customers to experience the vacation during the purchasing process, also an informational source for moms planning their family vacations. The site also includes pictures of rooms, restaurant information, tours of the facilities, entertainment schedules, and directions.

Terry Whaples, president of Nickelodeon Family Suites by Holiday Inn, must be doing something right. The Nickelodeon Family Suites Web site books more rooms than any other Holiday Inn property online. She emphasizes the importance of pictures on a Web site, particularly when it is intended to sell travel. Working off the success of catalogs that are so successful in capturing the attention of busy mothers, Whaples's Web site offers lots of pictures, including 360-degree tours. The tours allow moms to see exactly what they are buying in terms of family vacations. This type of approach will become even more important as Gen Y moms begin to shop for family items. They have grown up expecting to experience brands through multiple channels and senses. They not only want to read about a destination, but they want to see it in the most realistic state possible. It's important to allow younger mothers to experience your brand with as many senses online as technically possible.

MICROSITES/DESTINATION SITES

One way of creating specially designed online experiences is through minisites or destination sites. These online destinations may utilize an entirely different URL or may be hosted within your company's main site. They may contain special videos, music downloads, or interactive content. They are a great tool for targeting subsegments of your Mom Market, particularly with the younger media-savvy mothers.

Rachael Bender, cofounder of BlueSuitMom and Chief Technology Officer, explains best the opportunities marketers have to use minisites. Companies who want to market to Internet-savvy moms can take advantage by offering special destination sites that focus on a topic that is complementary to their products.

"Kraft uses the same strategy of informative time-saving content with product promotion on Kraftfoods.com. It offers a number of mom-friendly features, including online recipes, cooking tips, and promotions. But one of the best features is the meal and fitness planner. After you answer a few questions about your life, the site will develop a meal plan that includes a weekly shopping list, recipes, and recommended fitness activities. This feature keeps moms coming to the site to log what they eat into their food or exercise journal. The menu plan also reinforces using Kraft brands in the recipes," explains Bender.

She adds that smaller companies can use the same ideas to reach their target market. An example is the Web site for the Go Mom Planner, http://www.gomominc.com. Instead of just promoting where to buy the mom-friendly day planner, the site focuses on articles and tips to help moms make the most of their time through time-management techniques, organizational strategies, and ideas to help moms find balance. An added benefit to having a content-rich site is increased listings and higher rankings in search engines.

By creating content-rich specialty sites, companies can create the impression of being more than just a company that sells formula or cheese; it becomes a resource for helping moms manage their busy lives.

Microsites provide an excellent way to target specific niche groups. Wyndham Hotels has done a great job of targeting working women who travel for business through their minisite, http://www.womenontheirway.com. Cary Broussard, Vice President of Marketing for Women on Their Way®, explains the concept behind the site: "We created a social setting online that is relevant to the lives of our target audience. We give women business travelers a forum to tell us how to improve, submit ideas, and register for our annual contests." Broussard's efforts have been so successful that some of the ideas generated on the Web site have now been rolled out across the entire hotel chain.

Another marketing tool that is very effective in connecting with Generation Y moms is to challenge them to build their own sites within your Web site. Many photography destinations execute this strategy. They engage moms by providing the tools to build online scrapbooks, photo albums, and baby books. These minisites are then used to create an effective viral marketing tool for the host company. Because moms love to share, they distribute the URLs and passwords to friends and family with an invitation to visit the sites. Suddenly, a whole new group of prospective customers are now visiting the host company's Web site. It's a strategy that works well with the connectivity of Gen X and Gen Y moms.

Web Site Elements That Work for Attracting Moms

1. Recipes
2. Horoscopes
3. Salary comparisons
4. Baby namers
5. Gift suggestions
6. Message boards
7. Chat rooms
8. Expert questions and answers
9. Databases of definitions
10. Ideas for activities to do with their children
11. Medical explanations
12. Vacation planning tools
13. Checklists
14. Online calendar tools
15. Freebies

ELECTRONIC NEWSLETTERS
AND E-MAIL MESSAGING

There is no better cost-effective means of conducting a meaningful dialogue with mothers than through online communication. Moms have told us repeatedly that not only is this an effective way to speak with them, but its costs are modest and its returns are high when compared with the costs and the returns of traditional advertising. Moms spend an average of 86 minutes a day reading and sending e-mail messages, according to our research with Lucid Marketing. In the same study, 67 percent of moms said they check their e-mails three or four times a day. Examining their behavior online more closely, we learned that they are doing so almost every evening, throughout the day, and well into the night.

The electronic newsletter has taken the content from off-line publications and delivered it to moms in a personalized form that moms can read at their own convenience. The best newsletters from the standpoint of the reader include timely articles, quick tips, and special product offerings. For marketers, e-newsletters integrate product messages with valuable content and quickly link the reader to an online e-commerce destination. The best example of this is an article on bluesuitmom.com titled "Tips for Taking Your Child to Disney World." Recognizing that every mom dreams of experiencing Disney with her child for the first time but that the experience can be overwhelming for both parent and child, the article offers tips on surviving the day. It also offers product suggestions for making the day enjoyable such as an umbrella stroller or Pack 'N Play for the hotel stay. Every time the article runs as part of an electronic newsletter for a baby product site, sales for the products featured go up.

Electronic newsletters are not the only type of effective electronic messaging. Companies can competently communicate with moms online through personalized e-mails. One of the best features of electronic messaging is the ability for marketers to personalize the content. This is particularly appealing with the Mom Market because their needs change with the ages of their children. Moms tell us that e-mail messaging is effective in driving their purchases. In fact, 66 percent of mothers say they spend more money with companies that send useful and relevant e-mail messages that meet their needs. Seventy-one percent say e-mail messages influence their buying decisions, with 88 percent confirming that they make purchases based on e-mail messages. Kevin Burke, president of Lucid Marketing, describes the importance of personalization to mothers: "It's important to recognize each mom on an individual basis and to develop messaging and programs based on the individual mother's needs. Online technology has made it easy for companies to segment the Mom Market according to her individual needs." Burke adds that the payout for companies who make this connection with mom is big. "The better you relate to her, the better she'll relate to you and your company. More importantly, she'll remain loyal to you long term, which means greater sales in the future."

Burke's company has produced a number of successful electronic messaging programs targeted at mothers. One of the most successful is a program celebrating an important occasion for any mother—the birth of her child:

> We have a program that sends personalized and customized e-mail messages with a gift suggestion to moms 30 days prior to her child's birthday. The e-mail has a service focus, is a very soft sell for the product, and provides an easy way to buy the gift online. Then three days prior to the child's birthday, we send another e-mail message to the parent, but this one is a Happy Birthday E-Card addressed to the child. It is written for a child of that age to understand and appreciate. Humor is usually included as well as an online game or activity. There is no product or sales message—just feel good and best

wishes. Mom brings her child to the computer to show him or her that he or she got a Happy Birthday message from the brand—mom and child have a shared experience delighting in the message and upcoming birthday. And hopefully three days later mom is giving the child the gift we were promoting 30 days earlier.

Intuitively, we originally thought this was a strong program, but we really didn't appreciate how much of a positive impact it would have. E-mail message open rates as high as 70 percent and click-through up to 49 percent. But what really grabbed us was to have purchase rates increase by 28 percent and brand loyalty scores increase by more than 30 percent from this program alone.

Electronic messages via e-mail can also be an effective means of creating a buzz within the Mom Market. Eighty percent of mothers say they forward messages to friends if they find something of value within the message. During the 2004 holiday season, we created an e-mail campaign with the help of Lucid Marketing for Disney's direct-to-video release, *Mickey's Twice Upon a Christmas*. The e-mail offered moms the opportunity to have a personalized letter from Mickey and Santa sent via e-mail to their children at no cost. Our strategy was to provide moms with a valuable offering that could be carried offline as they shared the unique letter with other moms and family members. The e-mail was branded with the characters from the movie title to create brand awareness and drive the purchase of the DVD and video. The result was overwhelming as thousands of moms forwarded the free offer to other moms within their network and printed multiple copies of the letter for baby books and scrapbooks.

Technology allows marketers to get creative and connect with moms on multiple levels. We do, however, offer a few words of advice before you begin to utilize electronic messaging to moms. First, make sure you ask for permission. Just as she expects her children to ask before doing something, so she expects this of advertisers. Not only must you demonstrate your good intent by asking, but federal regulations now require it. Second, once you are given permission to send her e-mails, make certain that they are of value to her. If she feels like you are wasting her time or there is no benefit for her by opening your e-mails, she will simply push delete.

ONLINE CONTENT

Although we have already discussed content as it relates to organizing it on your Web site, we think it's important to take a deeper look not only at what goes into producing great content but at all the uses it has for marketing to moms.

In the early days of the Internet, there seemed to be a scramble to include as much content as possible without regard for quality or relevance. Today, wiser content managers will tell you that the quality of the content is as important as the quantity, particularly when it comes to mothers. Because most moms are searching for information that will directly impact the health and well-being of their families, they want to know that what they are reading is credible. The Internet has established an ocean of self-proclaimed experts so you want to make sure you are providing content that is backed by a reliable resource. This doesn't mean you must hire only Ph.D. writers, but you do need to find writers who have an established audience and a name that is trusted even if it's only one of their peers. In fact, sometimes a peer can be your best online expert.

Once you have the right writers, you must make sure they are penning the right words. As discussed earlier, moms want quick tips, good advice, and relevant content. In your lifestyle topics section, take an extra step in her shoes to offer something she didn't expect to find on your Web site, just as Fisher-Price did when it gave moms ideas for birthday presents and offered them tips for throwing parties, too. Do some of the work for her; take lots of choices and whittle them down to a top ten list. Give her new ideas that save time or help her with a challenge that is universal to all moms. If you are targeting a younger generation of moms, make your content easy to share by adding the E-mail to Friend feature or allow her to Instant Message it to another mother. If it's an article on home decorating a nursery, give her tools to design her own nursery online. Allow your content to come alive.

Finally, don't think that your content has to reside only on your Web site. If it's good content, share it as a mom would share good information. Offer your content to other Web sites who either share your target market or want to broaden the depth of their Web sites. We call this strategy GuerillaMomMarketing™. For our clients, we have established a network of mom sites whose publishers accept content for their sites that add value for their audience. Through carefully managed relationships, we have been able to build a system of mid- to high-level mom-related sites that offer us more than five million page views a month. It's important to recognize that there are thousands of viral communities of mothers out there with a high level of affinity to the sites they visit. Although Web sites such as iVillage.com will give you huge numbers in page views with one audience, it's sometimes even more effective to place your content on ten smaller sites with higher loyalty in their visitors.

Regardless of where you place your content, make sure each piece outside your URL has a link back to your Web site and is branded some way either within the article or in a byline. We saw a good example of this recently with Sprint. It teamed up with a woman who was an expert on staying connected with your children. Together they produced "Top ways to stay connected when apart from your child." The expert gave her advice and, as expected, one of the tips was to outfit your child with a Sprint phone. Although it had a commercial plug within the context of the article, it was still a good piece of information for on-the-go families. Sprint electronically sent the article to thousands of sites offering free use of the article as long as it linked back to Sprint.com. It was great for content-starved web-masters who are always looking for good material to refresh their sites with and it was an excellent way to increase traffic to Sprint.com. A similar campaign for o.b. Tampons recently ran, but instead of content it sent out links to a minisite that offered free samples of a new tampon. Many small sites added the link to their Freebie listings and produced traffic to o.b. Tampons for little investment.

WIRELESS APPLICATIONS

To explore the world of possibilities that exist in wireless ap-plications, we turn again to Rachael Bender, our CTO. "Beyond creating Web sites targeted to topics your potential customers find important, the next step is to connect with them on their mobile phones. Some researchers predict that in the next ten years, mobile devices will overshadow the use of personal com-puters for Internet usage," explains Bender.

A poll by Telecom Asia Pacific reports that mobile phone users are interested in online banking, stock market updates, shopping, mobile coupons, e-mail, directory searches, video-conferencing, and the ability to watch TV.

TV shows such as *American Idol* have already proven the ef-fectiveness of using mobile devices to connect with consumers. They've successfully used phones to promote voting, sweep-stakes, and program updates to constantly put their brands in front of the consumers. Some phones even now have the abil-ity to display live TV.

Bender says mobile phones and wireless-enabled personal digital assistants (PDAs) can help connect you with customers near your brick-and-mortar store. "When a mom passes by Toys R Us or McDonald's, you can display a special sales message or discount coupon," explains Bender. She adds that 88 percent of mobile users would be receptive to receiving electronic coupons for brick-and-mortar stores on their cell phones, according to research funded by Nokia and conducted by HPI Research Group. The study found that 31 percent would welcome such marketing. One of the advantages of marketing through mobile devices is the ability of your customers to immediately react to your offer.

But companies need to think beyond just offering a coupon or displaying an advertisement. Companies need to find ways to help simplify a mom's life through technology. For instance, a food product company could offer recipes using its products made available to download through her mobile phone. A mom could select what recipes she wants and then a shopping list could be generated while she is at the grocery store. Already 63 percent of moms are using the Internet to find recipes, according to a 2004 survey by Opinion Research Corporation for America Online; as Internet-enabled mobile devices become the norm, companies will have to offer this feature to mobile users.

An educational company like LeapFrog could offer simple lessons made available on the mobile phones that could be used by a preschool-age child while mom drives him or her home from school or while waiting in a doctor's office. LEGO could offer branded games available on mobile phones.

Magazines and newspapers can offer the ability to read articles when a working mom waits at the airport for her next flight. Mobile users in Asia are already using their phones to read books and watch TV on the Internet.

Baby product companies can offer parenting videos on mobile devices to help mom view them as resources instead of just diaper or formula companies. You could even offer a service that would provide daily parenting tips. Some companies overseas (where mobile technology is years ahead of what is offered in the States) already offer subscription services for smoking cessation programs on mobile devices.

Overworked moms are already tapping into the Internet to help them stay organized through e-mail alerts and reminders, according to a 2004 study conducted by Opinion Research Corporation for America Online. Soon moms will have the same ability on their mobile devices. Companies can send reminders of birthdays while a mom is at the mall.

The survey also found that 67 percent of moms use the Internet for product research. Companies can provide product information through mobile devices for customers to access while in the store.

Technology can put you in places where a mom can interact with your brand in ways like never before. It gives you the opportunity in a cost-effective manner to develop an ongoing dialogue with her either through Web site content, electronic newsletters, or e-mail messaging. The right uses of technology will allow you to position your brand as a resource and partner in a mom's role as a parent or home manager. You can link your service to valuable content, deliver timely messages to her, and allow her to experience your company before she walks through your doors. Remember that you are not alone on the Internet so it's important to establish credibility quickly with your audience, deliver content and tools in a well-organized manner, and provide a valuable message that moms will want to forward to other moms in their peer groups. Technology can be one of the most powerful delivery channels your marketing team has to utilize. Choose wisely and you will find your way into the hearts of moms virtually everywhere.

13

CULTURAL INFLUENCES IN A MOM'S WORLD

Writing this book has been a virtual experience. We're both working women who run successful marketing services consultancies. Yet, at our core, we're mothers and consumers first. So naturally we get swept up in the intangible influences—those societal triggers or cultural movements that alter our attitudes or behavior.

We created this book together while living and working separately in two cities, Atlanta, Georgia, and Pompano Beach, Florida. A project like this wouldn't be possible without the technological resources that we take for granted. We didn't realize the full impact of how technology has allowed us to bring this book to life until we sat in a conference room during one of our roll-up-your-sleeves work sessions.

When three mobile phones began chirping at the same time, we noticed the array of devices scattered around the table. In addition to the phones, we counted two personal digital assistants (PDAs), two laptops, and a mobile DVD player. We were surrounded by technology and didn't realize until that moment how important it was to the way we live our lives. Mothers are surrounded by technology, which is profoundly shaping the way they manage their businesses, their homes, and their families.

Our research for this book better clarified our view of the intangible influences that are shaping moms' attitudes and opinions and we learned just how important technology is in that regard. We asked mothers to prioritize the greatest differences between their generation of mothers and the generation that preceded them. Overwhelmingly, all generations of mothers—including Gen Y—pointed to technology, with more than 75 percent of mothers (77 percent) placing the impact of technology higher than single-parent families (71 percent), societal dangers to children (70 percent), media influence (57 percent), or even state-of-world conflicts (49 percent).

TECHNOLOGY TRIUMPHS

Our experience working with consumer electronics companies and retailers has given us a chance to better understand how mothers define technology. For most, technology boils down to the three *e*'s: efficiency, enrichment, and entertainment. Even if mom doesn't work outside the home, she has a strong need for tools that allow her to multitask and to get to the end of the day with a sense of accomplishment. Unless mom works in a technology-oriented business, it's unlikely she's concerned about how it works and/or the number of pixels or gigabytes it has.

When it comes to technology, mothers want to know "What's in it for me?" They're quick to detect the benefits of technology and typically eager to find ways to use them in their lives. You can count on a mom to evaluate a product's worth by determining how it's going to improve her life or that of her family. Will a particular gadget make getting multiple schedules organized? Does it allow her to stay in contact with family and friends easily and readily? Does it shorten the amount of time or effort it takes to complete a project? Does it enrich the lives of her children?

Stefanie Long is an associate at The Haystack Group, the mother of two preschoolers, and the person in the office who keeps everyone current on the newest offerings in consumer technology. Everyone knows a Stefanie. She's the person who finds a savvy shortcut for getting things done, or at least done more joyfully by using technology.

For weeks, we passed her desk and noticed a little blue box with headphones. Occasionally, she'd plug the mystery box into her computer then pop it in her purse. Like everyone, moms want to be entertained. And moms in the know and on the go have discovered the world of digital audio players, or MP3s. Stefanie—our own technology maven—has introduced all of us to the wonderful world of audible.com. In a nutshell, audible .com and other similar sites represent the newest innovation of books on tape. Teens and young adults have been using the MP3 technology to download music on portable audio players, but in this case, books can be downloaded onto the mobile device for playback anywhere, anytime.

"Digital audio books allow me to actually enjoy what would otherwise be drudgery. Doing laundry or mopping floors are chores, but I don't resent having to do them if I can make that time more productive. I don't know many moms who have the time to actually sit down and read a book. This way I can keep up with the newest novels without the guilt factor associated with reading when other things need to be done," says Long.

When it comes to technology, marketers should be aware of the generational differences in attitudes and behavior toward technology. Many studies have been conducted that tell us what we already instinctively know. Generation Xers and Generation Ys have a greater comfort level with technology. As boomer moms mature and assume their new roles as grandmothers, the younger generation will be in prime-time motherhood. With that will come more innovative ways of leveraging the benefits of technology and even greater expectations for what it can and should provide. These women will be pushing technology and consumer electronics manufacturers to do more to help facilitate the lives they want to lead.

We asked Katrina Blauvelt, communications director for Philips Consumer Electronics, about the impact of technology on moms and the Mom Market. Blauvelt's viewpoint is similar to others in the industry who agree that companies have to recognize that marketing to mothers runs on parallel tracks: the product has to be authentic and of high quality. If it doesn't meet these two attributes, then the mom's likely to be frustrated and disillusioned. It's equally important to focus on her comfort level with the product. You have to help her get comfortable with the benefits a particular technology or device offers. Make the benefits the superstar or she'll end up walking away thinking, I don't need that . . . I've gotten along just fine without it.

An example Blauvelt shared is of a newly launched Philips digital video and photo recorder that fits on a keychain. "The benefits of home theater systems are pretty blatant—a television with clearer picture and larger format that simulates the moviegoing experience—that's understandable, especially for the Baby Boomer mothers who actively seek solutions to support in-home family entertainment. On the other hand, if you look at things like keychain devices that record 28 minutes of video, a Gen X or Gen Y mom might be more inclined to embrace that. A technology like that requires a new way of thinking about how to share memories," explained Blauvelt.

But don't count boomer or Silver Bird moms out when it comes to boning up on or staying abreast of technology and electronics products. The AARP Web site hosts a Gadget Reviews section that contains information on a dizzying array of items ranging from Audible Otis, the digital audio player offered through audible.com, and SanDisk CruzerMini to Sirius Satellite Radio and the Roomba robotic vacuum cleaner (http://www.aarp.org/computers-gadgets/).[1]

If you think back to the chapter about messages and images, we recall the importance of determining if you're marketing to mom as the woman or mom as the product gatekeeper for the child. As all mothers know from the pester power of their kids who absolutely must have the latest noisemaking, light-flashing gadget advertised on television, technology products aren't for adults only. But regardless of the intended user, mothers still evaluate technology using the three *e*'s.

In the case of children, the benefits of enrichment take precedence. LeapFrog is a leading manufacturer of children's learning products that has ingeniously tapped into the brains and hearts of Baby Boomer mothers and the Silver Birds who have an innate desire to ensure their children get every opportunity to succeed. LeapFrog markets its products with the message that knowledge leads to success. Every mom wishes her children to be successful in the endeavor of their choice and wants to believe she helped them reach their full potential. This is a potent message from a company that backs up its language with tangible benefits such as an educational advisory board comprised of experts in reading, writing, literacy, and learning methodologies, and the LeapFrog SchoolHouse, which publishes tools and curriculum content for use in prekindergarten through grade eight classrooms.

Technology products aren't intangible—we play with them, work with them—but what is intangible is how mothers begin to adjust attitudes and behavior as a result of the availability of technology. The world for mothers is more accessible, whether she perceives her world from a global perspective or simply from the perspective of her own country. Regardless, technology has profoundly impacted the way she parents, gathers information, conducts business, shops, and communicates. She can place an order over the Internet, hold a three-way call on her cell phone, organize her family's schedule using a PDA, listen to digital audiobooks, and take digital pictures on a keychain-size device then print them out or share them with friends and family through her PC. The net result of this is a wholesale shift in how she perceives convenience, applies her need to be productive, and evaluates the value of brands. Understanding a mom's comfort level and her usage of technology products is important, but it's vital to clearly understand what your product can do for her and deliver benefit-laden messages.

It's also true that with technology, the medium is the message. Moms of all ages are tuning in to messages through untraditional airwaves. OnStar, the leading provider of telematics services in the United States, has more than two million subscribers who appreciate the in-vehicle safety, security, and information services provided. Using Global Positioning System (GPS) satellite and cellular technology to link a car's driver to the OnStar Center, motorists can access real-time, personalized help 24 hours a day, 365 days a year. Who would have imagined it possible for mothers to tap into the security, sense of well-being, and downright convenience of this type of technology? General Motors has found an excellent balance in explaining the assets of an unfamiliar technology in a familiar context through real-life stories about consumers who have benefited from the OnStar service.

PASSING THE EDUCATION TEST

At least two or three times a month a marketer will call inquiring about the homeschool market. The question always starts the same way. "What do you know about the homeschool market?" That initial question progresses to "We've been thinking that we should focus on homeschooling moms." We appreciate that these niche-seeking marketers call because all too often we watch eager pros jump feetfirst into a consumer segment without taking the time to understand the factors that drive them to the common lifestyle of the niche. The homeschooling community received a great deal of attention after a homeschooled child won the national spelling bee. The media then uncovered that the first runner-up was also homeschooled, thus opening debate on whether these children were receiving a better education at home than mainstream children were at school. The sudden media attention did a lot to highlight this alternative form of education. With the ability to combine religious convictions, individual family values, and creative curricula, homeschooling is seeing a surge in popularity. Today, 1.1 million children are educated in their homes.[2] So back to the question we hear so often, "What do we know about homeschooling?"

First, we would agree that it is a niche that presents opportunities to companies who want to reach mothers. In fact, we see it as a segment that will continue to grow, particularly as hands-on Generation Y moms grow their families. These mothers possess traits that today's homeschooling mom, although older in age, exhibit. For instance, they have a tendency to hold conservative religious views, are traditional in their parenting, and place a high value on education. What differs in the homeschooling mom of the future is that she will possess a high level of optimism for society in general. Social elements such as crime and peer influences had been a big motivator in keeping children home during the 1980s and 1990s, but today's Gen Y female is more determined to be part of the solution to these factors rather than to avoid them.

This segment of mothers is perhaps one of the most defined in terms of sharing many similar characteristics. Some of them are good for marketers, while others need to be observed and treated with care. Not to quench the fire of eager marketers, it must be noted that these moms spend less than most other segments of mothers. Their commitment to stay at home and educate their children comes with financial sacrifices and often one income. They are very value-conscious and wise about their spending. As we mentioned already, they tend to be conservative in their religious beliefs. Often you can find large pockets of homeschoolers who are also active in their houses of worship. The latter acts as support systems for their educational decisions. Advertisers must be sensitive to their viewpoints or risk offending them. This is an extremely connected group of moms who have a strong network of relationships with peers and spend a great deal of time trading lesson ideas with other moms online and offline. This is a marketer's dream because these women trust each other and word of mouth is very active among them.

Opportunities in the homeschooling market are available for school-supply companies as well as for companies that offer organic foods, natural herbs, craft supplies, and home items. We have worked with several companies who have entered this market successfully. One was a travel destination that developed science curriculum, partnered with a local hotel, and offered special homeschool packages for families to travel and learn. It was a good strategy because these moms place a high value on experiential learning and the special value price fit their budgets.

MOVE TOWARD SIMPLICITY

An editor's note in a recent issue of *Real Simple* magazine reads, "If you are reading this magazine, chances are you are a well-educated, savvy woman who understands many complicated things, including money. The one thing you may not understand is how to find more time in your week to make the little improvements necessary to keep it all running smoothly."[3] Touché. The mother's dilemma is about too much to do and not enough time to get it done. *Real Simple* is one of dozens of media forms springing up to help Baby Boomers, particularly mothers, better manage the overscheduled, overcommitted lifestyles that delivered enviable financial rewards and the inevitable burnout of trying to have it all. But thanks to Generation X and Generation Y, there's a movement afoot toward simplification.

Some refer to it as simple living, voluntary simplicity, or living gently. Whatever name you choose, it's more complicated than it sounds. According to the *Merriam-Webster Dictionary*, *simplify* is defined as "to make less complex." A visit to Amazon.com will net more than 100 titles of self-help and how-to books with a derivative of the word *simplify* in the title, such as *The Simple Living Guide, Choosing Simplicity,* and *Keeping Life Simple.* These books ostensibly help moms and others make life less complex.

We have found, though, that while the advice is well intended, it all seems focused on suggesting new activities and more strategies for doing less. We like the idea of companies such as Go Mom Inc. that provide solid solutions for helping a mom streamline activities and focus on priorities that help her fulfill her potential as a woman and as a caregiver for her family. A new subscriber-based electronic resource, the Six O'Clock Scramble, is an example of this new trend. The site provides a weekly e-newsletter with five healthy dinner recipes, with side-dish suggestions, that can be made in 30 minutes or less, along with a printable grocery list that can easily be modified. Pharmacies and dry cleaners around the country offer drive-through service, and taking things one step further, 1-800-DRYCLEAN picks up laundry at a customer's home, with options to schedule weekly or monthly stops and downloadable stain alerts. The notion of simplified living is one that works across generations. Generation X moms have incorporated simplified living in the way they are constructing their work lifestyles, which is exemplified by the number of home-based businesses these women are piloting.

Mothers we talk to tend to agree that the hectic daily pace of today's childhood might be getting out of hand. "A child who is constantly involved in all types of structured activities may not have the time to engage in important developmental activities such as self-reflection and self-evaluation," said clinical child psychologist Rob Heffer in an Associated Press article. A 1998 University of Michigan study found that children under the age of 13 had less free time (about 16 percent less) than they did a generation ago.[4]

A group called Family Life First, which refers to itself as a grassroots effort, was created to draw attention to the need to reduce the impact of overscheduling on children and to encourage quantity time and quality time with parents and family. Family Life First was kicked off with a lecture by Professor William Doherty of the University of Minnesota and author of *Take Back Your Children,* who shared the results of his research and expertise in studying family rituals.[5] The opportunities associated with tapping mothers' rituals are discussed in greater detail in the following chapter. As a result, we see a trend among moms to limit children's extracurricular activities and encourage family time at home. Game manufacturers are already on board with this idea.

Hasbro initiated the Family Game Night idea in 1999 and backed it up with a strong marketing campaign that helped the company earn strong sales for their game lines. In addition, families across the country began to incorporate games into their at-home rituals. In fact, Denny's, the largest full-service family restaurant chain, introduced in the summer of 2004 the D-Zone at Denny's for kids, featuring a new kids' menu with healthy options and Hasbro's most popular board games at tables to encourage family interaction.

MOTHERS AND SOCIETAL SAFETY

We heard regularly from mothers in group discussions and one-on-one that chief on their list of concerns about raising children today are the threats that are present on street corners and across the globe. Following the 9/11 tragedy in 2001, that concern ratcheted higher, with mothers and grandmothers listing dangers to children an issue that is harder for mothers to address today than it was for mothers of the generations before them. In our research, more than three-quarters of mothers (76 percent) stated that dangers to their children was the hardest thing about being a mother today, followed by media influence (53 percent) and the struggle to maintain balance between working and staying at home. Interestingly, Silver Bird mothers were the generation most concerned about today's risks to children, with 83 percent commenting on this danger.

For marketers, the concern about children's safety in the broadest form is an area that must be tread on carefully. There is a fine balance between promoting relevant messages of safety and alienating moms with messages laced with fear. A good example of the need to balance sensitivity with the delivery of pragmatic safety information is the proliferation of child safety identification and DNA kits. Dozens of companies are promoting kits containing ID bracelets and photo cards to DNA collection to parents, with a special emphasis towards mothers.

The National Center for Missing & Exploited Children directs visitors to dozens of these companies on its Web site and it even has a partnership with ChoicePoint, a leading provider of identification and credential verification services, where medical examiners and coroners can submit DNA samples for analysis and comparison. Needless to say, this is a touchy subject for mothers who are naturally concerned about the welfare of their children, but can find it overwhelming to emotionally attach to a brand that represents their worst nightmare. Companies that associate with nonprofit organizations, such as the National Center for Missing & Exploited Children, intelligently use that relationship as a vehicle to address moms' fears in a calm manner.

TRENDS IN HEALTH CARE

Our decades of experience in studying women, especially mothers, have given us a longitudinal perspective about the increasing importance of health care among mothers. Health care used to be something that only mature mothers were concerned with, but contemporary moms—regardless of their age—have a heightened awareness of the effects of nutrition and exercise on their health and that of their families.

Baby Boomer mothers are dealing with the health care issue on two fronts: addressing their own natural aging process and concerns about the physical well-being of their children. Visit http://www.ivillage.com and you'll come face-to-face with one of the top Web sites dedicated to women's issues. The site is chock-full of message boards, ongoing discussion groups, question-and-answer formats, and static information about women's health issues, ranging from difficulty conceiving to managing depression to dealing with the diabetes epidemic.

With heightened media attention on all that ails us, mothers are more than ever the gatekeepers for family health. As a result, they're taking health care into their own hands. Moms are attacking their own health with the South Beach, Atkins, and Fat Flush diets; Pilates-till-you-drop classes; and scores of supplements to get healthier and stay there. But what is driving this hoopla over health?

Let's start first with moms addressing their own health needs. With societal pressures to look young, feel young, and act young, mothers today face sometimes unrealistic expectations for their bodies. With reality programs such as *The Swan* and *Extreme Makeover* dominating the television listings, there seems to be no excuse for being unattractive anymore. Even the ugliest duckling can get a nose job and a tummy tuck and have her husband fall in love all over again. And taking the promised benefits of regular exercise to heart, Baby Boomers are working it out, for the physiological rewards in addition to the physical. With major medical advancements over the past two decades, people are able to stay healthy longer, and feel younger than their actual ages. In surveys, many people now don't consider midlife over until age 70, if ever.

In an article published in the *Eagle Tribune* of New England in 2003, Susan Whitbourne, a midlife expert at the University of Massachusetts Amherst, said that today's Boomers and Silver

Birds are physically working to turn back the clock.[6] Those who can afford it are successfully putting off the physical changes of age. In a time of fertility treatments, Botox, hair dyes, and Viagra, many of the physical restraints of aging no longer hold us back. Every cosmetic company on the market has introduced products focused on stalling or reversing signs of aging and more arrive on the market each day. Whether a mother shops at a prestigious salon or her local drugstore, antiaging products are readily available, pushing a message that she can do something about how old she looks. Waiting until their 30s or 40s to start a family is no longer a sure road to adoption for today's mothers-to-be and defining their cohort by life stage instead of age makes many seem younger in behavioral patterns and lifestyle choices.

Preventive measures are also important as Boomers and Gen Xers, hoping to push off age-related diseases until the bitter end, explore publications such as *Prevention* and *Self* to learn about the best foods to eat, the right exercises to do, and the appointments with doctors they shouldn't put off. Mammograms, skin biopsies, and hormone tests are being performed in record numbers for today's mothers who are prepared to take action if problems arise instead of burying their heads until it may be too late. And not content to take their doctor's advice alone, today's mothers are seeking answers to health problems or ways to prevent them with alternative therapists in areas such as acupuncture, biofeedback, and energy therapies. In the United States today, 36 percent of adults, mostly women, are using some form of complementary or alternative medicine, according to a study released in May of 2004 by the National Center for Complementary and Alternative Medicine (NCCAM) and the National Center for Health Statistics (NCHS), part of the Centers for Disease Control and Prevention. Products that have natural ingredients or designations are increasing in popularity with mothers.[7]

Turning attention to their children, mothers have their work cut out for them. According to the American Obesity Association, today approximately 30.3 percent of U.S. children (ages 6 to 11) are overweight and 15.3 percent are obese. For adolescents (ages 12 to 19), 30.4 percent are overweight and 15.5 percent are obese.[8] The epidemic of obesity is commonly thought to be the precursor to a large-scale diabetic epidemic that has already started to impact the types of food and medical products available at local grocery stores.

Mothers are starting to get messages about the importance of physical fitness, balanced meals, and stress reduction for their children. With concerns about harmful additives and fast-food fat content, and the trend toward "greener" meals, the overall U.S. market for organic foods and beverages advanced 81 percent from 2001 to 2004 to reach more than $5.3 billion, reports Dow Jones.[9] Mothers, seeing the health of their children as a direct reflection on their parenting skills, have taken matters into their own hands. Wealthy mothers now pay for personal training sessions or child-size exercise equipment to give their children a fitter future.

Brands that recognize the new sense of urgency mothers are giving to rightsizing their children, even stalwart sugar cereal and snack cracker brands, have changed their formulations to omit trans fats and excess sugar. Brands and companies that position themselves as aids in the fight against childhood illness will meet with better results than those who use scare tactics or negative associations to spur action.

14

OPPORTUNITIES FOR THE FUTURE

Janet Jackson must be a client at heart. Her hit, *What Have You Done for Me Lately,* asks the question every marketing professional must answer. The key to success in marketing to a new generation of mothers is to understand who they are and the things that influence them, and also to tap in to where they're going, keeping pace with their changing needs and wants so that they aren't left wondering what your brand has done for them lately. We wrote this book to direct attention to the importance of marketing to mothers, but more importantly, to understand them in multiple dimensions. We've introduced our belief that mothers should be segmented more by the age of their children and their life stage than the chronology of their particular generation. We've explored the influence that each generation of mothers has on those before and after them, and learned about the vital nature of intergenerational connections. Mothers are heavily influenced by their own mothers, and, as such, choose to follow a particular path in their own parenting styles, lifestyle choices, and purchase preferences, all the while unaware of the legacy that drives them.

We know from a trip through history books that the women we tend to consider traditional moms subtly, but surely, ignited the women's movement by serving their country in factories across the country. The baton was picked up and carried by the generation of mothers of the Baby Boom generation who saw an opportunity to prove their mettle in America's corporate halls . . . and the pendulum began to swing. We find now that the pendulum is swinging again as Generation X moms are collectively building a new framework in which they can parent—much the same way their grandmothers did—but with the benefit of a salary. We are anxious for new studies that will reveal more about the state of grandmothers today and will rely on experts in this area, such as Dr. Jean Giles-Sims, to help us understand the dynamic relationships Baby Boomer grandmothers will have on Generation Y and Generation Z offspring. And it goes without saying that we'll all be tracking statistics about grandmothers as primary or secondary caregivers for their grandchildren.

We've described how critical it is to understand if your brand, product, or service is best suited for a mother because it helps her prosper as a woman or because it provides another opportunity for her to be a better mom. Your messaging and use of imagery must be precise in this regard or you'll quickly be deemed irrelevant by thousands of women. Companies such as Mathis Dairies and programs such as Fit For 2 have done a good job of building relationships with mothers through sensitive, meaningful, discerning advertising, and public relations and direct marketing programs, which help to solidify the importance of their products and services to moms. And who would have imagined that the Internet would be among the top three sources of information for a mother, either health care– or commerce-related. And, finally, as Malcolm Gladwell described in his best-selling book, *The Tipping Point,* movements among groups of people can be kick-started by "people who influence us just because we have the occasion to come across them. And people whom we go to for information. I think that word of mouth is something created by three very rare and special psychological types, whom I call Connectors, Mavens, and Salesmen."[1] Visit any playground in America, take part in one of the thousands of organized playgroups taking place daily, or eavesdrop on an impromptu conversation in a supermarket aisle and you can see and hear the power of word of mouth and intangible influences. We've yet to meet a mother who isn't a connector, maven, or salesperson, and most moms are all three.

While we wish we had a crystal ball and could foretell exactly what moms will be doing during the next five years, we can provide some insights into the trends and opportunities that we think could prove to be productive assets for anyone who wants to build relationships with the Mom Market.

In our effort to forecast, we pay particular attention to Baby Boomer mothers because of their sheer size, purchasing power, influence on generations before and after them, and their staying power. Boomer mothers are an established force, many entering the world of motherhood more than 30 years ago and others becoming first-time moms just now. First-wave Baby Boomers are becoming grandparents. Some are even great-grandparents. Now that's a sobering thought. What is important is that they provide us with perspective and context in order to identify opportunities to create preferences for our brands with Boomers and the new generations to follow. And remember, our focus is about the life-stage impacts of these moms, whether a mom is a 25-year-old with two infants or a 50-year-old with three teens.

FLEXIBLE WORK OPTIONS

We've committed a great deal of attention to the subject of how mothers today are reengineering work styles, eager to balance their innate need to contribute and produce with their maternal need to nurture and provide for their children. While this is a hot topic among Gen X mothers, this approach is important as well to tail-end boomer mothers who waited to have children. Marketing to mothers isn't always an externally focused function; marketing to mothers within an organization should be the starting point. Children's Healthcare of Atlanta is one of the leading pediatric health care systems in the country and a not-for-profit organization whose staff of 5,500 is 80 percent female. The average age of women staff members is 37, prime time for childbearing and child-raising. To attract and retain top talent across the organization, Children's created several innovative programs that are positively impacting the bottom line by reducing turnover at key exit points, such as following maternity leave, and giving working moms benefits that keep them interested instead of entertaining offers for a few thousand dollars more in salary. "Our approach to employees is the same as our approach to patient care," says Donna Nazary, Director of Total Rewards for Children's Healthcare of Atlanta. "Because there is a shortage of clinicians in health care, we need to differentiate ourselves as an employer of choice, in particular to working mothers who make up such a large percentage of our workforce."

Children's offers benefits such as the compressed workweek, part-time hours, and three on-site childcare centers. These benefits are becoming more commonplace in female-dominated sectors, but Children's is pioneering some unique benefits that are resonating with its employee-mom audience. Each quarter, Children's hosts a baby shower, open to expecting moms or those going through the adoption process, that features guest speakers covering topics from finding childcare to how the Family Medical Leave Act benefits work. Attendees view a fashion show of branded Children's maternity clothes and get tips about proper car seat installation and safety from Children's Community Health Development & Advocacy representatives. In addition, Children's offers a $10,000 benefit to employees undergoing infertility treatments or pursuing adoption after six months of employment. A benefit for adoption, says Nazary, is highly unusual. To help ease the transition back into the workforce following maternity or adoptive leave, or to offer actively parenting moms more flexibility, Children's is piloting a telecommuting program as well as a new scheduling system that would enable staff members to build their own schedules electronically, determining exactly how many hours they want to work and when. In addition, employee feedback also provided the catalyst for a program being explored that would offer backup childcare for mildly ill children or for parents whose childcare has fallen through.

Each year, Children's gives employees a satisfaction survey, and the scores for loyalty and satisfaction are among the highest in the national health care industry. "We know we're doing something right," says Nazary. "If you're focused on the success of your organization, you have to have employee buyin." Her advice to marketers responsible for recruitment and retention: "Ask the right questions to know what your employees want, develop the programs, and communicate them properly to make your organization stand out to talented working moms."

Intuitive and in-touch companies recognize that the trend of the reengineered work style is here to stay, and instead of asking mothers to alter their needs, they're creating new ways to attract and retain valuable employees through outsourced job functions. In 2001, 25 million American workers reported working at home at least once a month as part of their primary jobs.[2] Of those, 19.8 million—15 percent of the workforce—reported working from home at least once a week. In 2001, 15.2 percent of women performed work at home at least once a week. Overall, workers are more likely to perform telework if they have children under 18. If you take a closer look, mothers with younger children (under age 6) were more likely than mothers with older children (ages 6 to 17) to telework—17.6 percent versus 16.0 percent.[3] Mothers choose to telework because of the flexible nature of this work style, providing a mechanism that allows them to attend to family-related issues and mirror their children's schedules with no commuting downtime. Companies that evaluate the success of their customer-service programs through productivity measures are reporting good news about the benefits to the organization of teleworking. A study of American Express employees found that teleworkers handled 26 percent more calls and brought in 43 percent more business than their office counterparts. According to *Call Center Magazine,* Jack Heacock and Associates, a call center and telework consultancy based in Colorado, demonstrated that home working can save more than $10 million over a five-year period compared with employer-premised call centers. It's not surprising that home-agent contracting is becoming a popular option. What organizations such as Children's Healthcare of Atlanta recognize is that mothers today, especially younger mothers with infants and school-age children, seek out and are finding work opportunities that match their custom-fit work styles. Gone are the days of 9 AM to 5 PM; say hello to the era of 5 PM to 9 PM, or noon to 5 PM or 11 PM to 6 AM.

RECONNECTING WITH THE PAST

One of the most frequent comments we hear from mothers who are entering their 40s or 50s, specifically those who are facing an empty nest in the near future, is that they feel pulled toward their roots—to products or activities they enjoyed in their youth. It's easy to understand that these mothers are yearning to reconnect with themselves after years of focusing their attention on their children and families. Many mothers view this desire for nostalgia as a safe, comfortable means to reenergize and transition into their next life stage, one that most likely doesn't require them to focus their full attention on children. Dorothy in the *Wizard of Oz* clicked her red heels three times and uttered "There's no place like home." Realtors across the country are repeating this line as Baby Boomers line up to right-size their homes and moms are leading the charge. According to Zhu Xiao Di of the Harvard Joint Center for Housing Studies, "Many empty nesters have the financial and physical assets to live it up." So Boomers are stepping into homes that meet their new lifestyles by making a move to larger, more expensive homes, investing in vacation homes, remodeling current homes, or moving altogether to communities developed for active adults. And they're putting their own unique touches to these new living spaces that offer throwbacks to their youth, incorporating a 1950s diner motif in a kitchen or a hobby studio where they can reconnect with their untouched paintbrushes.

The nostalgia cravings of boomer mothers are designing a new entertainment menu. A burgeoning backlash against saucy television content and reality programming is driving reruns of popular family entertainment programs and spurring the development of nostalgia-heavy new content. Entirely new broadcast networks, such as GSN, formerly the Game Show Network, are springing up to address these needs with vintage programming. GSN runs oldie but goody game shows like *What's My Line?*, *To Tell the Truth*, and *Beat the Clock*. Even youth-oriented networks like the WB are introducing programming with boomer appeal. *Jack & Bobby*, a series about, you guessed it, two charismatic brothers involved with politics, is laced with political reminiscence. The drive for nostalgia can be found on every American roadway, coast-to-coast, through boomer-inspired automobiles like the retooled Ford Thunderbird and last year's reintroduced Pontiac GTO. And it's not only testosterone behind the wheel. Finally, boomer mothers who recall a fondness for the home appliances of their youth can acquire vintage models, like the Frigidaire Custom Imperial Automatic Washer, at http://www .classicappliances.com. Part of a new print campaign for Turning Leaf Vineyards uses a play on the word *turning* by featuring an image of two thirtysomething or fortysomething friends enjoying a glass of wine as they are "turning it back" by looking through old photos and mementos with fondness. The past is never far behind, and today's mothers are bringing it closer.

According to its corporate Web site, American Girl is one of the nation's top direct marketers, children's publishers, and experiential retailers. Mothers will tell you that the American Girl doll ranks as one of their favorite purchases for their daughters. A frequently used example of boomer nostalgia, American Girl, LLC first tapped into the mother mentality in 1986 with the launch of a catalog of quality products for every stage of a young girl's development. *American Girl* magazine was added to the lineup in 1992, followed by a series of contemporary dolls. The company has successfully brought the American Girl experience to life for young girls across the country and their mothers through a totally integrated marketing experience, leveraging the impact of print and online media, books and proprietary retail stores, and in-store events. The company understands the impact of the integrated marketing experience for mothers—regardless of age—and smartly packages and promotes its offerings in a way that makes moms feel good about spending $100+ on a doll.

Even Gen X moms are feeling nostalgic as they become parents themselves, leading a rebirth of 1980s classic toys like Cabbage Patch Kids and CareBears. But unlike when they were kids themselves, they won't wait in toy store lines to get the hot retro toy. Gen Xers will get it when they want it, at online retailers or auction sites like eBay.

SHOPPING AT HOME

Avon, Tupperware, Mary Kay, and The Pampered Chef are all brand names that have been around for decades. All got their start and became established household names by tapping into what was, in their day, a revolutionary marketing concept:

in-home selling parties. Stay-at-home moms were presented with the opportunity to connect with friends, earn spending money, and, for many, dip their toes in the world of commercial enterprise for the first time. According to the Direct Selling Association Web site, in recent years, the popularity of in-home selling parties has grown tremendously. Several companies have explored this approach and found great success, like The Pampered Chef. In 1980, Pampered Chef founder Doris Christopher was looking for a career that would allow her to stay at home with her two daughters and earn extra money. Following one of her life's passions, Christopher began marketing cooking utensils and recipes. However, without capital to open her own store, she and her husband decided to promote products through in-home selling parties. Christopher recounts, "I can say from the moment I realized that I could redefine the direct-selling technique, I plowed straight ahead."

After a good run, the notion of the at-home selling party became passé and was replaced by catalogs and in-store experiences. As all things come full circle, in-home selling parties are back full force. Working moms are looking for social opportunities outside the office to network and meet other women with similar interests. Stay-at-home mothers are looking for the same, and the hosts, like their predecessors, find these opportunities suitable income generators. In addition to the pioneers, names like Southern Living and The Body Shop have extended the reach of their brands by extending into in-home parties. *Southern Living at HOME* was created in 2001 as an extension of the already established home accents and lifestyle magazine. According to the company's Web site, the party plan company is "committed to help entrepreneurs realize the dream of owning their own business and achieving personal and financial freedom." Binney & Smith, Inc., manufacturer of Crayola crayons and other kid-friendly brands, launched their own in-home selling business—Big Yellow Box—in June of 2004, and according to a company representative the venture has been highly successful.

The Tupperware party was the forerunner to what marketing professionals today refer to as viral marketing, which relies on an influencer to tell her friends about a product or service, and, in short order, a message is spread. *The Tipping Point* author Malcolm Gladwell describes viral marketing like a meme, an "idea that behaves like a virus—that moves through a population, taking hold in each person it infects." Gladwell uses the example of children's television shows *Sesame Street* and *Blue's Clues* as vehicles that started learning epidemics in preschoolers.[4] We find examples of viral marketing campaigns everywhere, but we believe the most impactful for reaching consuming mothers is through the current epidemic of the in-home selling parties. Today, the ultimate in-home party features a food poisoning–causing toxin. Botox injections are the fastest-growing procedure in the industry, according to the American Society of Aesthetic Plastic Surgery (ASAPS). For some medical practitioners, Botox parties are a key element of Botox marketing in the United States. According to ABCNews.com, sales of Botox, made by Allergan, Inc., are expected to jump 35 percent this year. The viral nature of the Botox party circuit is establishing this procedure as one of the most popular elective cosmetic surgery procedures in the country.

CUSTOMIZATION

Twenty years ago, Burger King gave us permission to have it our way, helping to establish a burgeoning trend of customization that nowadays can be found in every facet of a consumer's life. The offer of customization begets the demand for customization and that requirement is especially true among mothers. Starbucks has perfected the made-to-order, individualized coffee drink. The American Girl company will make a doll in your daughter's image and ship it right to your door. The United States Postal Service is getting in on the game through its licensed vendor Stamps.com. Stamps.com Inc., the leading provider of Internet-based postage services, is offering PhotoStamps, valid U.S. Postal Service postage stamps that are individually personalized with digital photographs, designs, or images. Moms can upload pictures, edit the images, and even add colored borders for one-of-a-kind mementos of family events or their children's artwork. At kiosks in malls across the country or online from home, parents can choose a CD that has their child's name in every song, like the Kids Music Box, http://www.kidsmusicbox .com. By registering with babycenter.com, pregnant moms can get weekly newsletters that depict the details of each stage of pregnancy, news she can use, and product content insinuated into the mix. After she gives birth, the newsletter focuses on her baby, giving developmental information, clever content, and more age-appropriate products, and the newsletter continues to grow as her baby becomes a toddler and preschooler. Greeting her by name, the newsletter demonstrates knowledge about exactly where she is in her role as mom. In terms of real-time communication, you can't get much more real. However, the push for customization isn't only for those who have young children now, as high-end retailers are smartly tapping into grandparent spending as well.

But how do mothers define customization? More broadly than we might suspect. They are seeking products and services not only to reflect their personalities and tastes, but to be delivered in a format and in a time that's of their choosing. In entertainment, we need look only to TiVo and Netflix. TiVo enables viewers to watch what they want, when they want. In fact, a recent ad in a popular food and lifestyle magazine depicts a woman who selects celebrity chefs to assist her in the kitchen when she's actually ready to be in the kitchen. With Netflix, by paying a set fee per month, moms can search by decade, special interest, or title for movies that get mailed directly to their homes in packages with return postage. They create a queue of movies they want to see, and get recommendations for flicks they might like. When they send one back, they get the next one on their list. The only store they visit is online and there are no late fees to dictate when they watch them. Customization that puts them in charge is key, and perhaps nowhere is that more obvious than with the cable companies' new offering: on-demand viewing. Far from something that only appeals to mothers, this concept is a big hit with children as well. Cranky dinner hour with the kids? Nothing on TV and tired of all the children's DVDs you own? Look at On Demand for vintage *Mr. Rogers' Neighborhood* episodes on PBS Kids or a favorite program from Nickelodeon. Later, mom can watch a new movie release with a small fee added to her cable bill, or watch all the recent *Sopranos* episodes. She can pause it to take a phone call, or stop it until her friend comes over to watch the rest.

From special ring tones to differentiate between her husband, mother, and best friend, to the custom publications like Kraft's *food & family* that print her name on the inside cover, moms today clearly are living in a custom world. And their children's worlds will be even more customized, from all aspects of room decor that can bear their initials or names to having their own "cubby" for virtual artwork on http://www.noggin.com.

THE BIRTH OF YOUR MARKETING OPPORTUNITIES

Customized experiences are also important, as mothers look for unique ways to make memories with their children. Retailers and party planning resources that help mothers create unique party packages that others in their class won't be having are in demand as birthdays represent one of the most important days of the year to demonstrate their commitment to their children. And with the burden of travel planning falling most often on the shoulders of moms, travel agencies and tourism bureaus would do well to offer customized vacation packages based on the ages of children in the family and the interests of its members. New journals, technology tools, and guides help moms get the most out of a custom vacation and preserve the memories she is hoping to create.

But from the experience perspective, the ultimate form of customization that we've found focused on children is the educational experience, when selecting private schooling or homeschooling, or when it comes time to choose a college. With parents frequently footing the bill, all aspects of the educational experience need not be founded only on helping the child achieve, but also on making it a positive experience for parents as well.

The need for customization extends beyond the need to provide moms with unique products or services. Marketers must apply the same elements of customization to the marketing plan they create to tap the Mom Market. The most successful strategies will communicate with moms in a way that clearly tells them that you understand them and are relevant to their life stages, lifestyles, and generations. Moms are as unique as the numerous combinations of marketing tools you as a marketer use to communicate with them. Apply the insights we've shared based on our extensive experience and ongoing research among the Mom Market with facts you gather about your target market and best customers to identify where your greatest opportunities lie to establish a meaningful conversation with moms. Remember, it's not about having a monologue with her, she wants and demands a meaningful dialogue with the brands she patronizes. She wants to nurture a relationship with you just as she nurtures her children and desires you to be a partner with her in her role as a mother. Marketing to moms is in reality marketing with moms in order to tap the tremendous spending power of these women with children. Every day another child in the United States is born, not only giving birth to a new mother but creating a new opportunity for marketers to win over the heart of a mom as a consumer.

INTRODUCTION

1. "Top 100 Countries GDP (Per Capita)," http://www.nationmaster
   .com (accessed September 14, 2004).
2. James Bennet, "Soccer Mom 2000," *New York Times,* April 9, 2002.
3. Center for Women's Business Research, *Women-Owned Business in
   the United States, 2002: A Fact Sheet* (Washington, D.C.: Center for
   Women's Business Research, 2002), http://www.nfwbo.org.
4. U.S. Department of Agriculture, *Expenditures on Children by Families*
   (Washington, D.C.: GPO, June 2001).
5. U.S. Bureau of the Census, *Population Projections of the United States
   by Age, Sex and Race: 1995 to 2050* (Washington, D.C.: GPO, 2000),
   http://www.census.gov.
6. Center for Women's Business Research.
7. Ibid.
8. Ibid.

CHAPTER 2

1. U.S. Bureau of the Census, *Population Projections of the United States
   by Age, Sex and Race: 1995 to 2050* (Washington, D.C.: GPO, 2000),
   http://www.census.gov.
2. Norman B. Ryder, "The Cohort Approach: Essays in the measure-
   ment of temporal variations in demographic behavior" (1951 thesis
   on file with University Microfilms, Ann Arbor, Michigan). Repub-
   lished under the same title (New York: Arno Press, 1981), adapted
   from a 1951 study by Norman B. Ryder, "The Cohort as a Concept
   in the Study of Social Change," 30 *AM. SOC. RREV.* 843 (1965).
3. Kingwood College Library, "American Cultural History," http://
   kclibrary.nhmccd.edu (accessed August 11, 2004).
4. Maddy Dychtwald, *Cycles: How We Will Live, Work, and Buy* (New
   York: The Free Press, 2003), 13.
5. Mark Trahant, Editorial, *Seattle Post-Intelligencer,* June 20, 2004.
6. U.S. Bureau of the Census, *School Enrollment* (Washington, D.C.:
   CPS, October 2002), http://www.census.gov.
7. Mass Market Retailers, "What's in a 'Megahit,'" http://www
   .massmarketretailers.com/articles/Whatsin.html (accessed September 7, 2004).

8. Anna Rachmansky, "Walking the Line . . . ," *Footwear News,* September 22, 2003.

CHAPTER 3

1. U.S. Bureau of Labor Statistics, 2001, *Statistical Abstract of the United States* (Washington, D.C.: GPO, January 2002).
2. Ibid.
3. U.S. Bureau of the Census, *Characteristics of Unmarried Partners and Married Spouses by Sex* (Washington, D.C.: GPO, March 2000).
4. Ibid.
5. Peg Tyre and Daniel McGinn, "She Works, He Doesn't," *Newsweek,* May 12, 2003, 45–54.
6. Center for Women's Business Research, *Women-Owned Business in the United States, 2002: A Fact Sheet* (Washington, D.C.: Center for Women's Business Research, 2002), http://www.nfwbo.org.
7. Stephanie Armour, "Some Moms Quit as Offices Scrap Family-Friendliness," *USA Today,* May 4, 2004, A1–A2.
8. Center for Women's Business Research.
9. U.S. Bureau of Labor Statistics, 2001.
10. *Radcliffe-Fleet Project: The Life's Work: Generational Attitudes toward Work and Life Integration (May 3, 2000),* http://www.ncrw.org (accessed August 1, 2004).
11. Ibid. (U.S. Bureau of Labor Statistics, 2002).
12. Cynthia Griffin, Column, *Entrepreneur,* April 2000, 42.
13. Ibid.

CHAPTER 4

1. Kingwood College Library, "American Cultural History," http://kclibrary.nhmccd.edu/decade30.html (accessed August 11, 2004).
2. Brian Metzger, "Rosie the Riveter and Other Women World War II Heroes," http://www.u.arizona.edu/~kari/rosie.htm (accessed August 17, 2004).
3. Karen Peterson, "GenX Moms Have It Their Way; Daughters of Boomers Carve Out a Balance Between Career, Family," *USA Today,* May 7, 2003.
4. Cokie Roberts, *We Are Our Mothers' Daughters* (New York: HarperCollins Publishers, 2000), 199.
5. Damaris Christensen, "Baby boomer moms see their daughters as more successful in their professional careers than they are but few would trade places, according to new research presented Sunday at a gerontological conference," *UPI Science News,* Chicago, November

18, 2001. http://www.medserv.dk/modules.php?name=News&file
=article&sid=1235.

6. Hillary Rodham Clinton, *It Takes a Village* (New York: Touchstone, 1996), 11.

7. Stephanie Dunnewind, "Parents Shouldn't Coddle Their Kids, Experts Warn," *The Seattle Times,* March 3, 2004.

CHAPTER 5

1. U.S. Bureau of the Census, *Population Projections of the United States by Age, Sex and Race: 1995 to 2050* (Washington, D.C.: GPO, 2000), http://www.census.gov.

2. Ibid.

3. Ibid.

4. Ibid.

5. Susan Littwin, *"The Postponed Generation: Why America's Grown-Up Kids Are Growing Up Later"* (New York: HarperCollins, 1987), 7.

6. K. McClure, "Can Generation Xers Be Trained?" *Training & Development,* March 1997, http://www.bresnahangroup.com/articles (accessed September 14, 2004).

7. Kevin Ford, *Jesus for a New Generation* (Downers Grove, IL: InterVarsity Press, 1995), 259.

8. Ibid.

9. Agnieszka Tennant, "Pastor X," *Christianity Today,* November 11, 1996, http://www.ctlibrary.com/ct/2002/aug5/3.40.html (accessed September 14, 2004).

10. *2004 Direct Selling Growth and Outlook Survey Fact Sheet,* http://www.dsa.org (accessed September 14, 2004).

11. National Center for Education Statistics, http://www.nces.ed.gov (accessed September 14, 2004).

12. Pamela Kruger, "Guess Who Didn't Save for College," *New York Times,* March 8, 1998, http://www.newyorktimes.com.

13. John Gunn, *Generational Marketing* (New York: New York Society of Association Executives (NYSAE), September/October 2002), http://www.GunnMarketingPartners.com (accessed July 7, 2004).

CHAPTER 6

1. U.S. Bureau of the Census, *Population Projections of the United States by Age, Sex and Race: 1995 to 2050* (Washington, D.C.: GPO, 2000), http://www.census.gov.

2. Zell Center for Risk Research Conference Series, *The Risk of Misreading Generation Y: The Need for New Marketing Strategies,* January 25,

2002, http://www.kellogg.nwu.edu/research/risk/archive.htm (accessed September 14, 2005).

3. Claudia Smith Brinson, "Generation Y: the confident, the connected," *The State,* July 14, 2002, http://www.thestate.com (accessed July 18, 2004).

4. Zell Center for Risk Research Conference Series.

5. Peter Markiewicz, "Who's filling Gen-Y's shoes?", http://www .brandchannel.com (accessed July 3, 2004).

6. Ellen Newborne and Kathleen Kerwin, "Generation Y," *Business-Week Online,* February 19, 1999, http://www.businessweek.com/ 1999/199.htm (accessed May 12, 2004).

7. Neil Howe and William Strauss, *Millennials Rising: The Next Great Generation* (New York: Vintage Books, 2000), 23.

8. Gary Colen, "Generation Y: No Brand Loyalty, Only Self," http:// www.pwa-par.org/newsletter/generation%20y.htm (accessed July 5, 2004.

9. Jill Bensley, "Generation Y and Culture: Do They Care?", http://www .jbresearchco.com/GenYandCulture.html (accessed July 9, 2004).

10. John Gunn, *Generational Marketing* (New York: New York Society of Association Executives (NYSAE), September/October 2002), http://www.GunnMarketingPartners.com (accessed July 7, 2004).

11. Ibid.

12. Ibid.

13. Ibid.

14. National Center for Education Statistics, http://nces.ed.gov (accessed September 14, 2004).

CHAPTER 7

1. American Association of Retired Persons, *The AARP Grandparenting Survey: The Sharing and Caring between Mature Grandparents and Their Grandchildren* (November 1999), http://research.aarp.org/general/ grandpsurv.html.

2. Ibid.

3. Ibid.

4. Ibid.

5. Laura Tiffany, "Isn't It Grand?", *Entrepreneur,* May 1999.

6. U.S. Bureau of the Census, 1980 Census, *1997 Current Population Survey, Marital Status and Living Arrangements,* March 1997 (table 4), http://www.census.gov.

7. Ibid.

8. U.S. Bureau of the Census, *Grandparents Living with Grandchildren: 2000; Characteristics of Grandparent Responsible of Grandchildren by Sex,* brief, October 2003 (table 4).

9. U.S. Bureau of the Census, 1980 Census, *1997 Current Population Survey.*

10. Ibid.

11. U.S. Bureau of the Census, *Grandparents Living with Grandchildren: 2000.*
12. Ibid.
13. American Association of Retired Persons.
14. Ibid.
15. *The U.S. Mature Market: New Perspectives on the +55 Consumer,* February 1, 2003, 4th Ed., http://www.packagedfacts.com/product/display (accessed September 8, 2004).
16. Pamela Paul, "Make Room for Granddaddy," *American Demographics,* April 1, 2002.
17. Laura Tiffany, "Isn't It Grand?" *Entrepreneur,* May 1999.
18. Frank Kaiser, "Secrets of Successfully Advertising to Seniors," http://www.suddenlysenior.com/howadvertiseseniors.html (accessed September 8, 2004).

CHAPTER 9

1. *National Mail Order Association Fact Sheet,* http://www.nmoa.org/ (accessed July 14, 2004).

CHAPTER 10

1. Al Ries and Laura Ries, *The Fall of Advertising & The Rise of PR* (New York: HarperCollins Publishers, 2002).

CHAPTER 11

1. Surface Transportation Policy Project, *High Mileage Moms* (Washington, D.C.: Surface Transportation Policy Project, May 6, 1999).
2. Ibid.
3. Don Montuori, *Package Food Facts,* "Food Bars: A Small Package That's Leading to Large Profits," http://www.packagedfacts.com (accessed September 14, 2004).

CHAPTER 12

1. Pew Internet and American Life Project, "Women Surpass Men As E-Shoppers During the Holidays" (January 1, 2001), http://www.pewinternet.org (accessed July 13, 2004).
2. Ibid.

3. "Surfer Moms Number 31 Million," http://www
   .network-centriadvocacy.net (accessed September 14, 2004).
4. Cyber Dialogue, "Cyber dialogue finds women reluctant to shop
   online due to security issues," http://www.cyberdialogue.com
   (accessed September 14, 2004).
5. Ibid.

CHAPTER 13

1. American Association of Retired Persons, the Gadget Review
   Section, http://aarp.org/computers-gadgets.
2. National Center for Education Statistics, http://nces.ed.gov
   (accessed September 14, 2004).
3. Kristen van Ogtrop, Editor's Note, *Real Simple,* April 2004, 32.
4. Associated Press Newswires, "AS overscheduled kids," March 13,
   2001 (accessed September 10, 2004).
5. NPR: Talk of the Nation, "Analysis: Whether today's children are
   too busy with activities and have too little family time," August 29,
   2000 (accessed September 10, 2004).
6. Julie Kirkwood, "30 (or 40 or 50) isn't what it used to be,"
   http://www.eagletribune.com/news/stories/20030803/LI001.htm
   (accessed September 14, 2004).
7. National Center for Health Statistics (NCHS), "The Use of Complementary and Alternative Medicines in the United States,"
   http://nccam.nih.gov/news/camsurvey_fs1.htm (accessed September 14, 2004).
8. American Obesity Association, "Childhood Obesity, Prevalance and
   Identification," http://www.obesity.org/subs/childhood/
   prevalence.shtml (accessed September 14, 2004).
9. National Association of Convenience Stores, "Food Safety Concerns
   Causing U.S. Organic Food Sales to Grow," http://www
   .nacsonline.com/NACS/News/ (accessed September 14, 2004).

CHAPTER 14

1. Malcolm Gladwell, *The Tipping Point: How Little Things Can Make a
   Big Difference* (Boston: Little Brown & Company, 2000), http://www
   .gladwell.com.
2. U.S. Bureau of Labor Statistics, *Work at Home in 2001* (Washington,
   D.C.: GPO, March 2002).
3. U.S. Bureau of Labor Statistics, *Employment Policy Foundation tabula-
   tions* (Washington, D.C.: GPO, March 2004).
4. Malcolm Gladwell, *The Tipping Point.*